In this volume are found some of the most profc
read on the situation of Christians in the "disor.
East today. The diversity of prophetic voices, m.   ...,
reflects the rich experience of those who attendc ... ∠∪ı / annual Middle
East Consultation in Beirut. Here is brought together the very best in biblically
and theologically informed reflection on the challenges and opportunities
of Christian witness in this troubled region. As key themes are explored –
persecution, emigration and minoritization – we are confronted with the raw
reality of suffering and despair; and there are also some necessary correctives
to prevailing perceptions of the situation. But overall there are grounds for
hope and even joy in the continuing calling to followers of Christ to be his
agents of transformation in the Middle East.

Anthony Peck
General Secretary, European Baptist Federation

The Church in Disorienting Times offers unique regional dialogue on the
problems of suffering, emigration, hopelessness and being a religious minority.
Personal stories are combined with contextual conversations to offer the global
church rare insights into discipleship, faith and mission in difficult contexts of
the Middle East. Highly recommended not only for Christians in persecuted
countries, but also for those living in contexts of religious freedom such as
in the West.

Kang-San Tan
General Director, BMS World Mission

One reason the gospel seems strange to so many people in the west – including
Christians – is that its original hearers were mostly sore afflicted: politically
oppressed, economically marginalized, physically spent. The gospel was – and
is – good news to people who need more than merely good advice: investment
advice, marriage advice, advice on how to vote or choose consumer products
or decide which exotic locale to vacation in. To get a sense of how the gospel
actually rocks peoples' worlds – their conflicted, shattered, dangerous, hungry
worlds – take a read here. Jonathan Andrews has beautifully captured in these
pages the shape and texture and many voices of a remarkable conference that
took place in Lebanon in the summer of 2017. Here men and women speak
candidly and wisely about the cost, sometimes fatal, of discipleship, and about

the risks, often brutal, of speaking good news. They wrestle with questions of faithfulness in the face of torture and imprisonment. They talk about a joy and peace in Christ that defies earthly explanation. They speak of a hope worth suffering and even dying for. Buy a copy, and listen in. But be warned: it will mess with you. It will shatter all versions of the gospel that reduce it to merely good advice. Prepare yourself to meet the real thing.

Mark Buchanan
Associate Professor, Pastoral Theology, Ambrose University, Calgary, Canada
Author of *Your Church Is Too Safe*

IMES Series

The Church in Disorienting Times

To Annika

With thanks for your love
of Serves and being in the
Middle East at this time

Jonathan
June 2018

Langham
GLOBAL LIBRARY

The Church in Disorienting Times

Leading Prophetically Through Adversity

Edited by

Jonathan Andrews

Including contributions by

Martin Accad, Ramez Atallah, Elie Haddad, Yohanna Katanacho, and Ehab el-Kharrat

GLOBAL LIBRARY

© 2018 Arab Baptist Theological Seminary (ABTS)

Published 2018 by Langham Global Library
An imprint of Langham Publishing

Langham Partnership
PO Box 296, Carlisle, Cumbria CA3 9WZ, UK
www.langham.org

ISBNs:
978-1-78368-434-2 Print
978-1-78368-435-9 ePub
978-1-78368-436-6 Mobi
978-1-78368-437-3 PDF

British Library Cataloguing-in-Publication Data
A catalogue record for this book is available from the British Library

ISBN: 978-1-78368-434-2

Cover & Book Design: projectluz.com

Dedication

To IMES and all who are reaching out in dialogue with people of goodwill in the Middle East, to remedy injustice, oppression and discrimination throughout the region.

CONTENTS

Preface

You might not like these times, but these are the times you have been given." These are the words of Dr Gary Nelson, whom we will meet properly shortly.

The Middle East and North Africa (MENA) region is passing through an era of tremendous upheaval and change. The relatively recent "Arab Spring" (see Glossary) gave voice to the repressed cries of many across the Arab world for freedom of conscience and expression, but the initial euphoria has given way to the scourge of continual armed conflict and large-scale displacement of people. The region's longing for stability and freedom is portrayed daily by the world's media outlets as millions seek resettlement and a new life, while the turmoil continues within the region as external forces wage proxy wars through competing religious factions, leading to the senseless deaths of young and old.

While many of the Christian communities across the region might appear to be in a precipitous decline, there remains a heartening stirring among God's people to see the tumultuous changes as a portent of hope rather than an omen of disaster. This book seeks to capture that spirit of positive and sober engagement, calling on the world's Christ-followers to stand shoulder-to-shoulder with their brothers and sisters across the MENA region. It seeks to motivate and inspire more people in more locations to work for the alleviation of suffering, the restoration of justice and the transformation of local and national communities for the benefit of all.

The Middle East Consultation organized by the Institute of Middle East Studies (IMES), held at the Arab Baptist Theological Seminary (ABTS), Mansourieh, Lebanon, in June 2017, addressed several critical issues facing the church throughout the Middle East. Some of these issues have been evident throughout the history of the church in the region, particularly, perhaps, since the emergence of Islam in the seventh century. However, many of the issues have taken on new levels of significance given the socio-political and religious conditions of the twenty-first century.

The contents of that conference provided the material for this book. The various contributions, mostly by people from the region, have been adapted to produce a cohesive book. In many places, the material is presented using the voice of the contributor. Such sections typically begin with a paragraph written by the editor to mark the transition to a different contributor. I, the editor, trust that it is always clear whose authority and voice is being presented in each section.

This book covers four major themes: persecution and suffering, emigration, hopelessness and despair, and minoritization, which is the overt suppression or oppression of one group within society. For each theme there was a keynote presentation by a citizen of a Middle Eastern country, which was complemented by a critique from a national of a different MENA country and enriched by the stories of others in the region. Finally, for each theme, there was an analysis of the same topic outside the Middle East. Some of the latter presented a broad global overview; others took an in-depth look at one location. Other material from the conference has been embedded within the text, including the daily devotionals based on various psalms.

Many of the spoken presentations were complemented by written papers. The material that follows started from the written material. In several places, additional content given during panel-based question-and-answer times has been incorporated. The witness statements, two for each of the four themes, have been written by the editor. For some, names have been changed.

The Consultation had the title "The Church in Disorienting Times: Leading Prophetically through Adversity." The word "prophecy" is used here in several ways. It can simply mean predictions for the future, the logical conclusions of current practices. Old Testament prophets compared the reality they saw around them with God's revelation, pointing out what conformed to his character and desires for his creation and what did not. As such, they highlighted that God would bring judgment on wrongdoing and what this might look like. Equally, they noted that this was not inevitable; change was possible. "Prophecy" is used here with this meaning: calling for and working for transformation of society for the benefit of all.

One theme that recurs is seeking justice. This too is used in the sense of what is right in the eyes of God Almighty. In much of the Middle East this inevitably leads to confronting the laws of the country that are discriminatory. As Christians, we do not define right and wrong only by the legal code that we live under: we critique all such systems based on our understanding of God as revealed in Scripture. Calls for justice in the pages that follow need to be understood accordingly.

I trust that you, the reader, will be stimulated and challenged by the richness of what is presented. May it enhance your understanding of Christians in the Middle East, inspiring you to stand alongside them. In addition, I trust that you will hear God's call to you, as an individual and as part of various communities. What would he have you do in the situations that he has placed you in?

So, a pause for some thanks before we move to our introduction, written by myself and incorporating material by Ehab el-Kharrat, an Egyptian church leader and former member of the Egyptian Parliament, as well as insights from the devotional speaker, Gary Nelson (see Contributors).

Jonathan Andrews
February 2018

Acknowledgements

My thanks to all those who spoke at the Consultation in June 2017 upon which this book is based. During the event, I especially appreciated being part of the Listeners' Group, ably chaired by Mark Buchanan, as we sought to summarize each day's presentations. The highlights observed assisted greatly in shaping the summary of each chapter.

A number of people provided helpful comments and suggestions after reviewing drafts of various sections of this book, including many of the contributors as well as Mark Buchanan, Malcolm Catto, Gordon Grüneberg, Barbara Hall, David Hunt, Martin Leonard and Alison Pascoe. I am grateful to each of you.

My thanks also to Vivian Doub at Langham Publishing, whose encouragement and expertise I have greatly appreciated; to Elias Ghazal, who acted as my point of contact with ABTS throughout the editing process; to Elie Haddad and Martin Accad, who were always quick to respond to queries on points of detail; and to Arthur Brown, who was the inspiration behind turning the Consultation into a book. I am indebted to you all.

Finally, I acknowledge the support of my wife, Wendy, who first introduced me to the Lebanese people whom she lived and worked among during the turbulent 1970s. Her insights have ignited in me a passion to see the church in the Middle East stand tall in the midst of a sometimes disturbing and yet always exciting and challenging context, to the glory of God and the growth of his kingdom here on earth.

Jonathan Andrews
February 2018

Abbreviations

ABTS	Arab Baptist Theological Seminary, located in Mansourieh, Beirut
AUB	American University of Beirut
FoRB	Freedom of Religion or Belief
IMES	Institute of Middle East Studies
ISIS	Islamic State in Syria and the Levant (see Glossary)
KGB	Committee for State Security (translation to English from Russian)
MENA	Middle East and North Africa
NATO	North Atlantic Treaty Organization
NGO	Non-Government Organization
PA	Palestinian Authority
UK	United Kingdom
UNHCR	United Nations High Commission for Refugees
USA	United States of America

Introduction

On the night that he was betrayed Jesus said to his followers: "In this world you will have trouble. But take heart! I have overcome the world" (John 16:33b). These words are very relevant for these times in the Middle East. This book encourages us to understand the distress in the region and how it reflects and contributes to the situation in the world as a whole. It also illustrates how God is at work amidst the difficulties. One theme is how we trust Jesus when life is full of challenges, and what it is that has enabled some to reflect the beauty and glory of Jesus in the midst of suffering.

We live in disorienting times. One reason why many feel disoriented is the pace of change: it often exceeds our ability to learn and adapt. In other words, the pace of change is faster than our ability to respond to that change. Consequently, we live with the feeling of struggling to keep up, of being behind where we would like to be; we seem to be constantly managing a sense of failure.[1]

Many circumstances cause suffering, distress and challenges. Chapter 1 considers persecution and suffering. Since 2011 there have been wars in Iraq, Libya, Syria and Yemen as well as conflicts in parts of Egypt, Sudan and Turkey. The West Bank and Gaza Strip continue to be affected by Israel's political and economic control, with overt armed conflict affecting the Gaza Strip, in particular, on several occasions. Some Palestinians continue to live in places designated as camps seventy years after their forefathers were forcibly displaced. Sudan has suffered internal conflict over many years; estimates of the casualty figures vary, with two million commonly cited. Distress is region-wide. Minorities are often targeted, especially Christians and "Muslims of the wrong type." Amidst political protests and changes in Egypt since 2011 there have been violent attacks on church property and Christian people, and while the perpetrators have often been extremists, the governments have not been blameless. Corrupt rulers affect Christians as well as the rest of society. How should we, the people of God, respond? What is the balance between accepting injustice and fighting for the rights of Christians and others?

---

1. These observations arose in a conversation between Gary Nelson (see Contributors) and Steve Holmes, chair of the board of Tyndale University College and Seminary, where Gary is the principal.

Chapter 2 looks at emigration, which is one response to the persecution, suffering and distress across the region. We are well aware of the worldly drive for more money, possessions, a "better life" and the global trend of consumerism that is profoundly affecting the region. It is one prompt for people to emigrate from the Middle East. Abraham is a significant character in Judaism, Christianity and Islam (see Gen 12–25). He was a businessman with great integrity. He had spiritual and financial motives for migrating: he is an example of how motivations intertwine in complex ways. We need to be aware that there is a very real danger for the church in the continuing emigration of Christians from the region, especially those in positions of leadership. We need to ask what the calling of God is on our lives.

Chapter 3 examines hopelessness and despair: the feeling of nobody being present to provide support, of there being no comforter, no prophet and no hope. It examines the situations of some groups who have come to accept that the absence of hope is their normal reality. We review the biblical material on lament, of mourning with those who mourn. More positively, this chapter gives the story of an area that has been transformed from within by the steadfast, faithful work of a small number of indigenous Christians. We ask where hope can be found. Which other locations might be transformed by indigenous Christians?

Chapter 4 examines minoritization. This is not just being a minority numerically, nor is it being marginalized, ignored and left alone on the edge of society. Minoritization is about being overtly suppressed, oppressed, disempowered and having no voice within wider society. In parts of the Middle East various communities are minoritized, including Christians, Kurds, Yezidis, Shi'a, Sunnis and Druze (see Glossary). No community is immune.

We live in disorienting times. Nationalistic movements and secular movements are very far from God's way of ruling; yet they receive much support from both within the region and beyond. Many charitable organizations actively endeavour to support the poor. Some are Christian, others are Islamist and some generate support for extremists, including ISIS (see Glossary) and other jihadists. The Muslim Brotherhood (see Glossary) remains active in many places.

Globalization is affecting the Middle East and rising aspirations are one consequence. Arab youth is part of the global youth culture. Youth movements are asking for greater freedom and more dignity, and modern technology allows them to communicate and organize themselves in new ways. The pace of technological change is one factor underlying our disorientation: simply keeping abreast of developments is a major challenge for many.

In Egypt, Christians have the freedom to change their religion, to become officially recognized as Muslim. At present, Muslims are not allowed to become officially recognized as adherents of another faith: irrespective of what they believe they will be treated by the state as Muslims. Many desire an end to this overt imbalance within the legal framework and social fabric of society. In Egypt, at least, this is a subject that can now be discussed publicly. The same imbalance occurs in most Middle Eastern countries.

Many business people are harmed by corruption, which forces them to relate to the rulers in certain ways. In Egypt, it has been estimated that 60 percent of the economy is outside of full legal scrutiny. Many labourers have limited means of organizing themselves to seek improved terms and conditions of employment. Many professions are not officially registered. Many buildings are not registered, simply because due process is not available. These facts of society create imbalance.

Like us, Jesus lived in disorienting times. The Jewish people were ruled by a foreign power and culture; their language was not that of their rulers. The Jewish people were divided over how to react to this context. Some opted for isolation, godly isolation, displayed in their dress code and strict religious observance. The Pharisees were one such group. A second response was that of the Herodians, a group whose name is derived from that of Herod the Great. They built the temple and balanced freedom to worship in that temple with paying taxes to the rulers. As they did so, they maintained their own power and position. A third response was characterized by the Sadducees. They spoke well, politically and socially, without challenging the rulers; they were good friends to the rulers. Finally, there were the zealots: those who armed themselves to protect the people and sought to remove those whom they thought of as the occupiers and restore the Jewish people's statehood. In the present era they would be an armed group and the rulers would label them "a terrorist organization," while others would regard them as "freedom fighters."

Jesus was not part of any of these groups. He was, though, part of the community and he displayed his power to all groups on different occasions. He did not respond to violence with violence, adopting a profoundly non-violent response. He did not join an armed group nor resist Roman soldiers. What he did do was resist corruption and injustice, whatever the source. This led him into confrontation with the Jewish religious leaders.

The Middle East today faces similar socio-political dynamics. The rulers are regarded as corrupt, unjust and lacking legitimacy. Some groups respond by working with them in the hope of maintaining or enhancing their own perceived prestige, position and power. Others seek various forms of withdrawal or confrontation. The challenge for Christian leaders is deciding how and when to challenge the rulers, knowing that to be critical might lead to a backlash against them or their community.

Disorienting times bring new layers of complexity. There are three main levels of complexity. First, there is simple complexity, such as in cooking, when one must follow the recipe and the outcome will be as expected. Second, there are more complicated situations, such as rocket science. Here there are many recipes and formulas to follow. Yet, if everything is done correctly, the completed rocket will work as expected. Third, there are situations, such as raising a child, in which there are many variables, some of which cannot be controlled. There is limited consistency between outcomes and the actions performed; there are no guarantees of how the child will emerge.

We need to understand each situation we face: which model of complexity is applicable. Amidst these times, there are no stock answers or one-size-fits-all solutions. One implication is that we need to beware of a transactional view of theology: simply God and me. In complexity, we need the communal: God delights in us, not just in me. We, together, are part of his purposes within the chaos and complexity: we will be better served if we face disorienting times together.

Many of us need to recognize that we might be persecuted but we are not left alone: Jesus promised to be with us always. We need to ask: How can we be courageous enough? How can we witness to Jesus in our circumstances? How can we discern faith? How can we bring healing to our enemies? How can we be a prophetic voice? What does the Holy Spirit want to say to us today about peaceful resistance, challenging violence and critiquing Herod and Empire – that is, autocratic rulers? How can we follow Jesus's way?

How does one live with feelings of disorientation? Disorientation is often felt before it is described. Psalm 8 is a celebration of the God who delights in the psalmist and has a special purpose for him. Does creation make us feel small? Or does it make us realize how special we are to God? We need to allow God to be part of the questions as well as part of the answers.

Our first challenging arena for these questions is that of persecution and suffering. We begin with a succinct and dramatic summary of twenty centuries!

1

Persecution and Suffering

A cursory reading of the history of the Middle Eastern church reveals the enormous amount of tragedy, persecution and outright ethnic and religious cleansing experienced by Christians living in the region.[1] A succinct summary would start with the persecution outlined in the New Testament, which was followed by the Roman persecution under Nero and then Diocletian. There followed Persian, Jewish (in Yemen and Ethiopia, and during the Roman-Persian Wars), Islamic and Mongol (under Timurlane) persecutions. The Ottoman era included the massacres of Badr Khan, the Hamidian massacres and finally the Armenian, Assyrian (see Glossary) and Greek genocides of 1915. Persecution in modern times includes numerous instances in Iraq, Syria, Algeria, Libya, Tunisia and, as will be described below, Egypt.

According to Pope Benedict XVI, Christians are the most persecuted group in the contemporary world.[2] In 2013 the Holy See (colloquially, the Vatican) reported that over 100,000 Christians are violently killed annually because of some issue relating to their faith.[3] According to the World Evangelical Alliance, over 200 million Christians are denied fundamental human rights solely because of their faith.[4] Of the 100 to 200 million Christians under

---

1. E.g. Philip Jenkins, *The Lost History of Christianity* (New York: Harper Collins, 2011).

2. Pope Benedict XVI, "Religious Freedom, the Path to Peace," 1 January 2011, accessed 1 February 2018, http://w2.vatican.va/content/benedict-xvi/en/messages/peace/documents/hf_ben-xvi_mes_20101208_xliv-world-day-peace.html.

3. E.g. "100,000 Christians Killed Each Year Due to Faith," *The Commentator*, 30 May 2013, accessed 7 September 2017, www.thecommentator.com/article/3664/100_000_christians_killed_each_year_due_to_faith.

4. Godfrey Yogarajah, "Disinformation, Discrimination, Destruction and Growth: A Case Study on Persecution of Christians in Sri Lanka," *International Journal for Religious Freedom* 1, no. 1 (2008): 85–94; accessed 24 November 2917, www.iirf.eu/site/assets/files/91409/ijrf_2008-1.pdf.

assault, the majority are persecuted in Muslim-dominated nations.[5] Further, Christians suffer numerically more than any other faith groups or groups without a religious belief in the world. Of the world's three largest religions, Christians are, allegedly, the most persecuted, with 80 percent of all acts of religious discrimination being directed at Christians.[6]

Such claims and statistics are debated within Christian human rights circles. Clarity of definition is one aspect. For example, some include as martyrs all those who die whilst working in Christian activities abroad, even when the cause of death is a traffic accident.

We will begin our exploration of the twenty-first-century situation with a focus on Egypt provided by Ramez Atallah, head of the Bible Society of Egypt. His focus is on the long-standing Christian presence in the country where he was born, raised and has lived for the past thirty-eight years. As will become apparent later in this book, he has also lived in Canada, and Rebecca, his wife, whom we will meet in chapter 3, is Canadian by birth. Ramez's reflections explore religiously motivated persecution and discrimination, asking when the latter can be regarded as the former. They look at Jesus as our role model. When should injustice be challenged, and when might it be best to quietly accept it?

After looking at Egypt, we will move the short distance to a reflection on the situation of the Palestinian people provided by Daniel Bannoura, an instructor at Bethlehem Bible College in Palestine. He contributed the opening two paragraphs of this chapter. He broadens the topic from suffering specifically for being a Christian – religious persecution – to being part of a wider society all of which is being subjected to injustice. This changes the dynamics of how to challenge injustice, should one choose to do so, whether alone or with others. He begins our journey of developing a prophetic response to disorientation. In particular, he explores whether to quietly accept or overtly challenge the imposition of injustice.

Our witness accounts tell us the stories of two people who chose to follow Jesus Christ having been raised as adherents of another faith. Both experienced strong reactions to their religious conversions. This leads into our global cross-check which examines how the worldwide church should understand and respond to religious persecution in the Middle East and elsewhere.

---

5. Bruce Thornton, "Christian Tragedy in the Muslim World," *Defining Ideas*, Hoover Institution, 25 July 2013, accessed 23 November 2017, www.hoover.org/research/christian-tragedy-muslim-world.

6. Paul Vallely, "Christians: The World's Most Persecuted People," *The Independent*, 26 July 2014, accessed 23 November 2017, www.independent.co.uk/voices/comment/christians-the-worlds-most-persecuted-people-9630774.html.

We begin our journey in Egypt.

Reflections on the Christians of Egypt Today (by Ramez Atallah)

My purpose in this section is to relate the Scriptures and the recent history of Christians in Egypt to the issues of suffering, discrimination and persecution. The underlying assumption is that, while we should do all we can to work for justice and equality for all, we can be encouraged by the example of Egyptian Christians who have maintained a vibrant Christian witness for over two thousand years in spite of often being a discriminated minority.

Down through the ages the church has developed and articulated a "theology of suffering" which is deeply rooted in Scripture. This teaching on suffering and its practical ramifications has been expressed differently in the varied church traditions, yet all traditions are agreed on its centrality to Christian belief and practice.

In these pages, our focus is on suffering for the cause of the gospel. Many of the principles expressed are applicable to situations in which Christians suffer because they are part of a society that is facing injustice.

The cross is the main symbol of Christianity and represents suffering. Jesus used this symbol when calling his disciples to follow him by "carrying" their cross as he carried his.[7] Down through the centuries Christians have identified themselves as "the people of the cross" and have been willing to suffer and even die for that identification. While many from all walks of life and traditions wear crosses to testify to Jesus, Coptic Christians in Egypt tattoo a cross on their wrist to make sure they never deny their Lord! Some have paid with their lives because of that. The apostle Paul expresses this very clearly when he says that we are called not just to believe in Jesus but also to suffer for him.[8]

Those who claim Jesus as Lord and Saviour should "follow in his steps."[9] Since we follow a "man of sorrows" and a "suffering servant," our lives also will be characterized by sorrow and suffering.[10]

---

7. "Whoever does not take up their cross and follow me is not worthy of me" (Matt 10:38).

8. "For it has been granted to you on behalf of Christ not only to believe in him, but also to suffer for him" (Phil 1:29).

9. "To this you were called, because Christ suffered for you, leaving you an example, that you should follow in his steps" (1 Pet 2:21).

10. "He was despised and rejected by mankind, a man of suffering, and familiar with pain. Like one from whom people hide their faces he was despised, and we held him in low esteem" (Isa 53:3).

All Christian traditions have developed ways to help us remember how much Jesus suffered for us and how we can participate in or empathize with his sufferings. Many focus on the weeks leading up to Good Friday. Whether it is the "steps of the cross," passion plays, long Holy Week services or other ways, the purpose has always been to make sure faithful followers of Jesus feel and experience the depths of Christ's suffering on our behalf.

We suffer not only as Jesus suffered, but also because this is God's divine methodology to build in us the kind of character he seeks.[11] All Christian traditions have developed disciplines to help believers on the long road of Christian sanctification.[12]

It is only in recent years that some churches have embraced the "comforts of the world" to such an extent that many of these practices have lost their meaning and impact on character-building. One blatant example of this in Egypt is the vegan fast which Coptic Christians do on more than 210 days per year. Many, especially the poor, fast faithfully. However, some have developed a method that fulfils the letter of the fast but denies its spirit and intent.

We are admonished to look forward to suffering: just as Jesus endured the cross "because of the joy set before him,"[13] so we are called to yearn to be like him through suffering.[14]

In his sermon at the funeral of dozens of Coptic Christians who died in church buildings at the hands of suicide bombers on Palm Sunday, 9 April 2017, Bishop Rafael, the secretary of the Coptic Orthodox Holy Synod, said:

> True, we love martyrdom. But we also love life. We do not hate life on earth. God created us on earth to live, not die. The fact that we accept death does not mean our blood is cheap, and it does not mean that it does not matter to us. We do not commit suicide. But we witness for Christ, whether by our lives or by our

---

11. "Not only so, but we also glory in our sufferings, because we know that suffering produces perseverance; perseverance, character; and character, hope" (Rom 5:3–4).

12. Long periods of fasting and frequent daily disciplines of prayer have characterized much of Roman Catholic, Eastern Orthodox and Oriental Orthodox practice. Among many Protestants, matters of dress, abstaining from smoking and drinking, and regular daily devotions and church attendance have been seen as necessary disciplines.

13. "For the joy that was set before him he endured the cross, scorning its shame, and sat down at the right hand of the throne of God" (Heb 12:2).

14. "I want to know Christ – yes, to know the power of his resurrection and participation in his sufferings, becoming like him in his death" (Phil 3:10).

transition to heaven. If we live, we live for the Lord; and if we die, we die for the Lord.[15]

The deeply entrenched belief that martyrdom can be part of the cost of being a Christian, which Coptic Christians have held since the establishment of the church in Egypt, has been tested in a new way in recent years. On 15 February 2015 a video was released online showing the murder by members of ISIS of twenty Egyptian Christian labourers and a Ghanaian in Libya. The graphic video is thought to be the only one ever made of an actual martyrdom. The victims refused to denounce their faith and were, therefore, brutally executed. Their story became a great source of encouragement to Egyptian Christians to believe that this centuries-old understanding of martyrdom was still relevant for the twenty-first century. Instead of frightening or intimidating Egyptian Christians – as ISIS had intended – this video was the source of a real revival of true commitment to Christ among millions in Egypt.

Thus, regardless of all that the "health and wealth" preachers (see Glossary) claim, any Christian in the Middle East, or anywhere in the world, who lives by the principles of the gospel will, at some time and in some way, have to "suffer for Jesus."

So does the Bible's teaching on suffering mean that we should not work against discrimination and persecution of Christians? As in many other controversial issues among Christians, there are two extreme positions which have been articulated and practised during the past two thousand years. Some have misinterpreted this teaching as meaning we should pursue suffering as a virtue in and of itself, and thus never protest against injustice against believers. Others on the opposite end of this spectrum believe that their main mission in life is to fight for total equality and full justice for Christians (and others) at any cost. There are many positions at various points between these extremes.

Obviously we should not seek suffering and will rightly avoid it if we can. Equally, the fanatical pursuit of full justice and equality for all is fraught with intrinsic problems. Communism, socialism and many other ideologies attempting to establish ideal societies have ultimately failed.

Egypt is an example of the latter. When the country became a republic in 1952, the new rulers believed that the way to social justice was socialism. Being Muslims, they planned to implement Soviet socialism without communism's atheistic ideology. They began a massive program of nationalization, which

---

15. Taken from a spoken message by Bishop Rafael, General Secretary of the Coptic Orthodox Synod. Address during funeral for those killed on 9 April 2017.

included the state taking over many large privately owned businesses and operating them by and for the people. Alas, a new class of government bureaucrats emerged who used these businesses for their own personal benefit, bankrupting the companies in the process. Consequently, most of the businesses collapsed or needed constant government subsidies to keep operating. A new class of nouveau riche emerged in government employees, rooted in having exploited the poor.

My wife, Rebecca, has ministered for more than thirty-five years among Sudanese refugees and garbage collectors in Egypt. (This will be described in chapter 3.) Whilst these two groups of people are among the most discriminated against and oppressed minorities in Egypt, she finds more joy, love and faith among them than among our middle-class neighbours or church members who are not "oppressed" and live a relatively comfortable life.

So, while Christians need to do all they can to help correct injustices in society, we need to realize that this can never be our ultimate goal. We need to remember that economic and social freedoms do not, in themselves, provide the answer to humanity's deep yearning for real peace. People need to be changed from the inside by the power of the gospel to know their true worth as children of the Creator of the universe. Only then can they begin to transform their societies for the better.

We mentioned the suicide bombings of two churches on Palm Sunday 2017. In response, many Christian and Muslim activists blamed the government, with angry voices in the media demanding greater protection of Christians by the authorities. What these activists do not realize is that all the government has in its power to do in response to these demands is to tighten security. On this occasion, the President requested, and was granted by parliament, emergency powers to allow police to arrest suspects without having to obtain a warrant. This made some of these activists accuse the government of reducing human rights in Egypt.

What is a better way to respond to violent attacks? One approach would be to follow the lead of many liberal Muslim thinkers in Egypt who are calling for the elimination of those Hadiths (see Glossary) that are used by radical Muslims to justify violence against non-Muslims. This is not something that governments can legislate against even though they would like to do so. So lobbying the government to help alleviate the plight of Christians in Egypt usually results in more restrictions in society in general, which ultimately makes life harder, not easier, for Christians.

One response from individuals was public statements of forgiveness made by some of the bereaved. Several of the families of the victims of the ISIS atrocity in Libya 2015 made such statements. In April 2017 a mainstream, secular television news show broadcast an interview with the widow of the security guard at one of the churches attacked earlier that month. The lady expressed her pain, forgave the perpetrators and invited them to consider the claims of Christ. The news-show anchor remarked that Egyptian Christians love their country and "are made of steel." He noted that such forgiveness was outside his experience.[16]

Are Christians in Egypt Discriminated Against or Persecuted?

The confusing paradox is that Christians in Egypt today are, in my opinion, both a discriminated minority and a thriving community. It is true that many Christians are discriminated against in Egypt and some are persecuted. However, many Christian entrepreneurs have thrived in the post-Sadat neo-liberal economy since the early seventies. These Christian entrepreneurs now control a significantly disproportionate amount of Egypt's wealth. It is equally true that churches of all confessions are thriving and flourishing more than ever before since independence in 1952. While an Egyptian can credibly make such a generalization regarding Egypt, one wonders how many Westerners can make similar claims about their countries.

Though Egyptian Muslims respect Jesus as a prophet, tensions in Egypt have always existed between the Christian community and some of their Muslim neighbours. Such tensions are often linked to issues like building churches, religious conversions or rumours of cross-religion romances. These tensions can spill over into ugly violence, especially in rural or crowded inner-city areas where the rule of law is weak. In many cases, the police cannot or will not do much. One reason is because "village tribalism" often has its own rules and traditions which even a strong police force cannot overcome. Another is that most policemen are Muslims who may sympathize with those who are persecuting Christians.[17]

Muslim converts to Christianity in Egypt are persecuted by their families and harassed by the authorities if their families and/or neighbours lodge a complaint against them. They cannot change their official religion and this

---

16. See, for example, "These Egyptian Christians Are Made of Steel," YouTube, accessed 21 November 2017, https://www.youtube.com/watch?v=CXwTp0fCsgc, which surrounds the original Egyptian video with a church service in the USA.

17. One can read stories in the media of mobs burning Christian homes and chasing Christians out of mainly Muslim villages.

creates endless complications for them within the tightly knit society. While the authorities no longer detain them if they do not cause problems, they live in a constant state of uncertainty and fear. There seems to be very little the government can legislate in this matter at the present time.

While no Muslims want someone in their family to convert to Christianity, it is often forgotten that no Christians want someone in their family to convert to Islam. So both communities shun or persecute any of their members who convert or attempt to do so.

The situation in North Sinai in mid-2017 – which received some attention in the worldwide press – was unique and distressing. There we had a state of war involving very violent radical Muslim groups and Egyptian government forces, both the police and the army. The violent targeting of Christians was similar to what was happening to Christians in ISIS-controlled sections of Iraq and elsewhere. In this context, some of the North Sinai Bedouins (see Glossary) aligned with the extremists, whilst others worked with the authorities in an attempt to restore normality.

An Islam Soaked in Christianity

In the seventh century Egypt was one of the most solidly Christian nations which Islam conquered. All Egyptian converts to Islam were former Christians. So, since the Christian faith and practice were deeply entrenched in our country's heritage, Egyptian Muslims inherited from their Christian past many Christian values. Thus, Egyptian Islam was tempered by Christian values.

It was only in the 1960s and 1970s, when Egyptians went by the hundreds of thousands to work in Saudi Arabia and other Gulf States, that they were brainwashed by Wahhabi Islamist ideology (see Glossary) and brought this back with them to Egypt. Thus, while many Egyptian Muslims unwittingly hold on to some Christian values, the present official al-Azhar (see Glossary) school of thought interprets the Qur'an in a static and traditionalist way.[18]

In the Aftermath of the Arab Spring

Egypt was indelibly marked by the unexpected eighteen-day popular revolution in early 2011. Before 25 January 2011 only a few Christians were interested

---

18. E.g. Amr El-Abyad, "Has Al-Azhar Stifled Egypt's Intellectual Enlightenment?," Egyptian Streets, 27 July 2015, accessed 15 November 2017, https://egyptianstreets.com/2015/07/27/has-al-azhar-stifled-egypts-intellectual-enlightenment/.

in or knowledgeable about politics. Few Christians voted, and many had very little nationalistic fervour. Several years could go by without a pastor making reference to Christians' social responsibility except as it related to social needs in the church. The same was also true of the average Muslim Egyptian who was also not interested in politics.

However, 25 January and what followed changed this. For a long time after the revolution the main topic of conversation among Egyptians was politics. Newspapers and television stations gained large readerships and audiences among all walks of life. After the revolution several political writers and those who hosted political talk shows became well-known personalities. Before the revolution newspapers and television shows rarely involved women or Christians. After the revolution talk shows dealing with many different topics often included women and Christians as guests. The church became an integral part of Egyptian society in ways that we could not have envisaged.

During the January 2011 revolution, churches near places where violent clashes took place between demonstrators and police opened their facilities as field clinics to serve the wounded. Qasr al-Dūbārah Presbyterian Church, located just off Tahrir Square in central Cairo, pioneered this; they received the attention and admiration of the nation. Many pastors began encouraging their members to be involved in the political process. The Bible Society of Egypt had a campaign called "Rebuild Egypt" with banners, adverts in newspapers, and leaflets of Scripture selections all pointing to the Bible as a source of principles upholding the lofty aspirations of the revolution: freedom, social justice and human dignity.

Christians in a variety of social agencies and ministries were able to make their services known through the much greater exposure now accessible to them. The extent and appreciation of their work broadened, to the benefit of society. Some groups have been successful in hosting friendly yet frank interfaith dialogue between leaders of the two main religions.

In the early days of the Arab Spring, Egyptian revolutionaries really believed that a new era of complete openness and democracy was being ushered in. Alas, this new-found sense of freedom evaporated when the Islamists (see Glossary) rose to power. There was then no way to remove them except by popular demand. This is what happened on 30 June 2013 when Egyptians went to the streets in unprecedented numbers in the millions asking for the then President Morsi to step down. Morsi rejected the demands and the call to hold new elections. Egypt had no impeachment procedure in place at that time, so there was no way to remove him except through military intervention. The vast majority of Egyptian Muslims and Christians supported the removal of

Islamists from power and welcomed the subsequent election of former army general Abdul Fattah al-Sisi to the presidency.

The most remarkable development was not the rise of the Muslim Brotherhood to power – which was fearfully expected and shattered most revolutionaries' dreams – but rather the completely unexpected wholesale rejection of political Islam following the fall of its short one-year rule. Political analysts have referred to this as a modern-day miracle: nobody expected it.

Ironically, however, the only way found until now to keep the Islamic radicals at bay has been to dramatically increase and reinforce the powers of the police and the army. This has kept Egypt mostly safe from terrorist attacks but has put a stranglehold on the dreams of the many for more freedom, less police brutality and greater government accountability. This, in addition to the very serious economic near-collapse of the Egyptian economy and the devaluation of the Egyptian pound to half its former value, has made the revolution's slogan of "bread, freedom and social justice" seem like an unreachable goal.

While many Egyptians feel that their dreams for a freer and more just society have been shattered, most Christians feel more supported by their government than ever before. The obviously genuine intent of President Sisi to include Christians as full citizens has been a great encouragement. His strong stand against radical Islamic teaching, and his deep desire to reform the way in which Islam is practised, strikes a responsive chord among us. The disappointing fact, however, is that his many laudable initiatives find little positive response among the official Islamic institutions in the country. It is not that Muslim scholars are necessarily anti-Christian, but rather that the dominant school of Islamic interpretation has become the "literalist" one and this has made it much harder to reform the way in which the Islamic faith is practised. One clear example of this during 2017 was President Sisi's attempt to restrict the practice of oral divorce (see Glossary) in Egypt.[19]

The public discussion of these issues, precipitated by talk-show programs and the President's many comments, creates a slightly more open atmosphere which gives Christians limited hope that Egyptian Islam will become softer and more tolerant rather than harder and harsher in the coming years.

---

19. See "Egypt's President Al-Azhar in Opposition over Requiring Muslim Men to Inform Women of Divorce," 8 February 2017, accessed 31 August 2017, https://egyptianstreets.com/2017/02/08/egypts-president-al-azhar-in-opposition-over-requiring-muslim-men-to-informwomen-of-divorce/.

A Positive Picture

This approach will frustrate many. It will frustrate some Egyptian Christians who desperately want to leave their country for a better life in the West and to do so must convince themselves – and the countries which might grant them asylum – that life in Egypt is unbearable for Christians. It will frustrate some leaders of Christian ministries in Egypt who believe that their support from Western organizations depends solely on painting a picture of Christians in Egypt as a totally persecuted minority. It will frustrate Western fundraisers who have bought into and often exaggerated this persecuted-minority image of Christians in Egypt and have thus created for themselves a donor base of people who give with the wrong motives. It will frustrate Christian revolutionary idealists who had hoped for an Egypt with a Western model of democracy and feel that I [Ramez Atallah] am a compromising pragmatist who has sold out to the establishment.

Having studied and worked in Canada and the USA for eighteen years, being familiar with the day-to-day lives of close relatives and friends in North America today, and leading a thriving and growing Bible Society in Egypt, I am firmly convinced that the opportunity for serving Jesus faithfully in Egypt is much easier and more fruitful than in any so-called "free" Western country. True, there are many daily challenges in Egypt, but most are related not to our faith but to the complexity of life in Egypt.

For the past twenty-six years the staff of the Bible Society of Egypt whom I lead have been determined not to be discouraged by the many obstacles which face us. To use the language of open and closed doors (which will be explored in chapter 2), when a door is closed we look for a window to jump in through. We have managed to jump through many windows in the past twenty-six years and, by God's help, the ministry continues and expands.

Devotional Pause: Psalm 91 (by Gary Nelson)

On that positive note, we will pause and look at a psalm before considering a different perspective. The situation of the church in Palestine broadens our consideration to suffering as part of the whole of society, which gives a different dynamic when considering whether to accept or challenge injustice. The daily devotions were led by Gary Nelson and each was based on a psalm.

Psalm 91 has been described as a "psalm of perspective."[20] The psalmist paints a picture almost like a viewer of a film or an observer of a war from a safe distance, yet he describes something that he fears may happen to him.

Many of us live with these "what if it happens to me?" struggles. News channels broadcast a constant stream of bad news majoring on possible, but not certain, severe consequences. The challenge for us is to discern what is real and what is imagined.

Psalm 91 contains a tension. Does the psalmist believe that something bad will happen to him? By the conclusion of the psalm you find yourself in dis-ease, wondering whether he is living in reality or in a self-made fantasy. What is clear, however, is the writer's deep confidence and trust in God (v. 2).

A superficial reading of Psalm 91 suggests that we will come through disasters unscathed: an imagined reality consistent with neither the stories of those affected by ISIS nor other tragedies described in this book. The writer, however, is not suggesting that illusion.

The psalmist lists all his fears, those that are real, present and not suppressed. However, he is not consumed by these fears. He is aware of his situation. He knows that his fears are rooted in reality; they are not simply imagined. Some people are kept in constant fear, creating "self-fulfilling prophecies" as the fear induces choices that produce what is feared. The psalmist is not acting in this way: he is not obsessed with his fears. Instead, he is focused on God. Praise is woven throughout this psalm – for example, acknowledgement of God's faithfulness in verse 4. Hope is rooted in knowing that God is with us, and that he never gives up and he never lets go.

This God is always close because of who he is. He is committed to dwelling with us, to sharing our lives. So whatever I fear may happen or whatever does occur in my life is companioned by God and the promise of his companionship. That is the perspective captured in Romans chapter 8, where Paul describes our present sufferings and future glory. He concludes with the triumphant promise that nothing can separate us from the love of God in Jesus Christ (Rom 8:38–39). This is what it means to dwell in his love, "in the shelter of the Most High," and to live in the salvation that God provides for his people (Ps 91:1, 16).

---

20. Robert Doran, Leander E. Keck, J. Clinton McCann Jr. and Carol A. Newsom, *The New Interpreter's Commentary*, Vol. 4 (Nashville: Abingdon Press, 1996), 1046.

Cross-Check: Palestinians – Suffering Occupation (by Daniel Bannoura)

From Egypt we move to the Palestinian situation. As above, we will be guided by someone born, raised and living and working in the situation. Daniel Bannoura is a native and resident of Bethlehem, Palestine. He presents a brief survey of the situation of the church in Palestine and its place within a society that, in its own eyes, faces the daily struggle of living under occupation. He asks how the church should respond to injustice and he introduces a theological consideration of how to live in disorienting times.

The Situation in the West Bank and Gaza Strip

I begin with a brief summary of the situation on the ground in Palestine. The theme is that the Palestinians have been squeezed into a progressively smaller proportion of the land. Key steps in this process since the Second World War (1939–1945) include the UN Partition Plan of 1947, the declaration of the State of Israel in May 1948 and the Six-Day War of June 1967 when Israel occupied East Jerusalem, the West Bank and the Gaza Strip. The events of 1947–1949, referred to by Palestinians as the Nakba (literally, "catastrophe"; see Glossary), and of 1967 left many Palestinians displaced as refugees throughout the Middle East. The Oslo Accords signed in 1993 led to the creation of the Palestinian Authority (PA) and the division of the West Bank into Areas A, B and C based on where the PA and the Israeli authorities have administrative and security control. Area A has full PA control, Area B has PA administrative services with Israeli security control, and Area C has full Israeli jurisdiction.

In 2017 the Palestinians in the West Bank lived confined to a series of enclaves defined by these designations, movement among which was restricted by numerous Israeli checkpoints. This reality made no distinction between Muslims and Christians. One consequence was that Palestinians emigrated, something we will return to in chapter 2.

For Palestinians, the term West Bank typically means the area east of the Green Line, the widely accepted border with the State of Israel from 1948 to June 1967 (see Glossary). This includes East Jerusalem. Other definitions are used; for example, many Israelis use the term to mean the area east of what the Israeli government calls "the seamline security fence." This is the barrier, sometimes of barbed wire and sometimes an eight-metre-high concrete wall, that separates the West Bank from Israel. It runs along the Green Line in places and elsewhere cuts into what the Palestinians regard as the West Bank in order to ensure major Jewish settlements are on the western side.

There is some religious persecution. On 6 October 2007 Rami Ayyad was murdered, martyred, in the Gaza Strip.[21] This is very rare, as are other forms of bodily harm. The number of Christian Palestinians – including some of my own friends and neighbours – murdered by the Israeli Defence Forces far exceeds the tiny number of Christians killed by religious extremists. My main argument here is that Christian and Muslim Palestinians suffer together under an unjust military occupation.

Returning briefly to religious persecution, there is societal discrimination and pressure. Some Muslims have told Christians to leave on the grounds that the land should belong to Muslims. Other Muslims accuse Christians of not suffering under the occupation. We, Palestinian Christians, reject both charges and the ideology behind them.

One factor in these accusations is Zionist theology as promulgated by some Christians outside the Middle East, often referred to as "Christian Zionists." I summarize this as seeing the State of Israel as significant in eschatology. In Palestine, Zionism (see Glossary) is perceived as a nationalistic ethno-religious ideology, one of whose objectives is the complete territorial conquest of the West Bank and its inclusion within the State of Israel. Since most Muslims are deeply concerned about justice, Zionism is perceived as being contrary to local senses of justice and, consequently, it is off-putting for them: they distance themselves from Christians, including us, the Palestinian Christians. What many Palestinian Christians are seeking is a biblical, moral and just approach to our context. One subtle effect of Christian Zionism (see Glossary) is that it prompts distrust of evangelical Palestinian Christians within the wider Christian community. We find this profoundly unhelpful.

In practice, we have adopted a theology of survival, of staying. The struggle is to exist or not. We resist in order to stay, the alternative being that we disappear: non-resistance is not an option. We are part of the broader struggle against occupation.

A Palestinian Response to Suffering: The Kairos Document

One Christian response to the situation was the publication in 2009 of the Kairos Document entitled "A Moment of Truth: A Word of Faith, Hope and

---

21. Rami was managing a Christian bookshop in the Gaza Strip at the time of his murder. He left behind two children and his wife who was pregnant at the time.

Love from the Heart of Palestinian Suffering."[22] This document was signed by leading Palestinian Christians from a broad range of Christian traditions, denominations and churches present in Israel, the West Bank and the Gaza Strip. The following extracts give a flavour of the document:

> We, a group of Christian Palestinians, after prayer, reflection and an exchange of opinion, cry out from within the suffering in our country, under the Israeli occupation, with a cry of hope in the absence of all hope, a cry full of prayer and faith in a God ever vigilant, in God's divine providence for all the inhabitants of this land. Inspired by the mystery of God's love for all, the mystery of God's divine presence in the history of all peoples and, in a particular way, in the history of our country, we proclaim our word based on our Christian faith and our sense of Palestinian belonging – a word of faith, hope and love. (Kairos Document, Introduction)

> The mission of the Church is prophetic, to speak the Word of God courageously, honestly and lovingly in the local context and in the midst of daily events. If she does take sides, it is with the oppressed, to stand alongside them, just as Christ our Lord stood by the side of each poor person and each sinner, calling them to repentance, life, and the restoration of the dignity bestowed on them by God and that no one has the right to strip away. (Kairos Document, 3.4.1)

> The mission of the Church is to proclaim the Kingdom of God, a kingdom of justice, peace and dignity. Our vocation as a living Church is to bear witness to the goodness of God and the dignity of human beings. We are called to pray and to make our voice heard when we announce a new society where human beings believe in their own dignity and the dignity of their adversaries. (Kairos Document, 3.4.2)

> The aggression against the Palestinian people which is the Israeli occupation, is an evil that must be resisted. It is an evil and a sin that must be resisted and removed. Primary responsibility for

---

22. The Kairos Document: "A Moment of Truth: A Word of Faith, Hope and Love from the Heart of Palestinian Suffering," 2009, accessed 25 October 2017, http://kairospalestine.ps/index.php/about-us/kairos-palestine-document.

this rests with the Palestinians themselves suffering occupation. Christian love invites us to resist it. However, love puts an end to evil by walking in the ways of justice. Responsibility lies also with the international community, because international law regulates relations between peoples today. Finally responsibility lies with the perpetrators of the injustice; they must liberate themselves from the evil that is in them and the injustice they have imposed on others. (Kairos Document, 4.2.1)

We say that our option as Christians in the face of the Israeli occupation is to resist. Resistance is a right and a duty for the Christian. But it is resistance with love as its logic. It is thus a creative resistance for it must find human ways that engage the humanity of the enemy. Seeing the image of God in the face of the enemy means taking up positions in the light of this vision of active resistance to stop the injustice and oblige the perpetrator to end his aggression and thus achieve the desired goal, which is getting back the land, freedom, dignity and independence. (Kairos Document, 4.2.3)

Resistance to the evil of occupation is integrated, then, within this Christian love that refuses evil and corrects it. It resists evil in all its forms with methods that enter into the logic of love and draw on all energies to make peace. We can resist through civil disobedience. We do not resist with death but rather through respect of life. We respect and have a high esteem for all those who have given their life for our nation. And we affirm that every citizen must be ready to defend his or her life, freedom and land. (Kairos Document, 4.2.5)

Accept Injustice or Fight for Justice?

The Kairos Document asserts that the church will be involved in the struggle to address the injustice seen in the occupation. In this situation, the church chooses to confront injustice, not quietly accept it. This brings the church into political activities.

Here a tension rises between my thesis and the one that Ramez presented above. His tendency is towards working within Egypt's socio-political situation, whereas, in Palestine, Christian Palestinians are taking the alternative approach of overtly naming injustice and joining the struggle to resist it and seek change.

In Egypt, the status quo includes examples of bloodshed and discrimination for the Egyptian church in the post-Mubarak period. Is the Egyptian government so weak and incompetent that all it can do is to tighten security using procedures that violate basic human rights? One might suggest a myriad of laws that the Egyptian government could amend which would curtail violence against Christians in Egypt. These include reviewing the educational curricula in schools, limiting religious illiteracy among Muslims, secularizing laws to be based on citizenship and pressurizing al-Azhar into a better engagement with Christians. Palestinian Christians would be careful about giving implicit support to what looks to some to be a military dictatorship and to restrictions on human rights. Such support of the government, whilst strategic and protectionist for the short term, might seriously hamper the active ethical and prophetic role that the Egyptian church could play. And, more importantly, it compromises the prophetic voice of the church in speaking truth to power and in standing with the suffering against the perpetrators of injustice.

The Bible, together with a plethora of theological works throughout the ages, consistently views the pursuit of justice as an integral part of Christian living. In fact, justice is viewed by many Christians as a fundamental aspect of God's character. Furthermore, the biblical text makes it clear that the pursuit of justice is a core aspect of Christian mission. The following are a few of the numerous Old Testament passages that could be cited to support this view:

> Follow justice and justice alone, so that you may live and possess
> the land that the LORD your God is giving you. (Deut 16:20)

> How long will you defend the unjust
>   and show partiality to the wicked?
> Defend the weak and the fatherless;
>   uphold the cause of the poor and the oppressed.
> Rescue the weak and the needy;
>   deliver them from the hand of the wicked.
>   (Ps 82:2–4)

> Learn to do right; seek justice.
> Defend the oppressed.
>
> (Isa 41:17a)

> He has shown you, O mortal, what is good.
> And what does the LORD require of you?
> To act justly and to love mercy
> and to walk humbly with your God.
>
> (Mic 6:8)

This theme continues in the New Testament, as illustrated by the following passages:

> A bruised reed [my servant] will not break,
> and a smouldering wick he will not snuff out,
> till he has brought justice through to victory.
> In his name the nations will put their hope.
>
> (Matt 12:20–21, quoting Isa 42:1–4)

> And will not God bring about justice for his chosen ones, who cry out to him day and night? Will he keep putting them off? I tell you, he will see that they get justice, and quickly. (Luke 18:7–8a)

> [the prophets] through faith conquered kingdoms, administered justice, and gained what was promised; [they] shut the mouths of lions, quenched the fury of the flames, and escaped the edge of the sword; [their] weakness was turned to strength; and [they] became powerful in battle and routed foreign armies. (Heb 11:33–34)

It is evident from a cursory reading of these passages that justice is viewed as an essential part of God's nature and his dealings with humanity. Further, the pursuit of justice is a fundamental requirement of biblical Christian living: it was practised by the prophets of old, and decisively and finally by Christ. Today's church, especially in the Middle East, needs to pursue justice fanatically – by which I mean, with relentless, determined persistence.

While this position is biblical, this should be only one part of our theology of suffering. True, the cross represents suffering; but it also represents much more, including "Christus victor," God's justice and atonement. Christians should imitate Jesus in their suffering, but also in their tireless efforts in making the kingdom of God a reality on earth "as it is in heaven" (Matt 6:10b).

Towards a Theology of Responding to Suffering

While some suffering is allowed by God to build our character, suffering is also inflicted on the believer unjustly (e.g. the book of Job). Sometimes suffering is undeserved and brings with it no redemptive quality; for example, genocides and earthquakes.

The response of the Coptic church to the attacks of August 2013 and Palm Sunday 2017 was remarkable in its courage, unconditional love and relentless forgiveness. At the same time, we need to critically examine the practical ramifications of these attacks on the church. While many Christians decisively chose to love and forgive their enemies, have not these attacks also produced despair and hatred among some? While the clergy of the church have admonished the believers not to fear martyrdom, have not many left Egypt for the West and elsewhere in order to escape potential martyrdom? (This will be explored further in chapter 2.)

The resilience of the Coptic church is a magnificent lesson for the regional and global church. However, Christians need to be careful not to insist that this attitude is essential as the one and only reasonable and effective fact on the ground. A prophetic response to suffering, an adequate and prophetic theology of suffering, needs to address every aspect of suffering – emotional, existential, psychological, theological and philosophical. That is the only way the church today can sustain its presence and witness in the MENA region.

The church has a role in addressing and critiquing the systems of power in any society, especially the structures of oppression. Being prophetic necessarily requires a deconstruction of "the powers that be." Consequently, the church in each location needs to carefully and prayerfully reconsider its relationship to the authorities, especially those that are dictatorships. This is not easy. One aspect that must be acknowledged is that what is possible changes over time and varies by country. In disorienting times, this dynamic can change repeatedly. (This will be discussed further in chapter 4.)

For Palestine, the context includes critiquing Christian Zionism, as noted above, and its counterpart, Jewish Zionism.

The church also needs to consider its relationship with Muslims and Islam. At times in the Palestinian context, this has been dysfunctional. Today, the church needs to be critical yet contextual and charitable, especially towards the political Islam present in our society. (This will be discussed in chapter 4 and the appendix.) In the Palestinian context, Christians and Muslims suffer together under occupation. We can, and should, work with those willing to work with us in addressing issues of injustice that affect our whole society.

Witness 1: Aydin – A Convert Who Was Obliged to Leave His Country

We will add to our theological reflections of leading prophetically in adversity after considering the stories of two individuals for whom following Jesus proved costly.

Aydin was born in a Central Asian country (see Glossary). His conversion to Christianity led to severe persecution which prompted him to leave his country, travelling via Russia to Norway. Subsequently, he moved to Istanbul, where he works among people from Central Asia. He is persistent in encouraging people to remain faithful to Jesus whatever their circumstances.

The Central Asian countries were part of the Soviet Union (USSR) for eighty years. During this period, Christianity was severely repressed. The situation changed with the demise of the USSR and the granting of independence to Aydin's country in 1991. The population is overwhelmingly Sunni Muslim. The first known conversions to Christianity occurred in 1992.

Aydin's upbringing had been difficult and he felt deeply empty, a situation that endeavouring to be a good Muslim failed to address. When he was seventeen he visited Moscow, where he met one of the first converts to Christ of the same ethnicity who happened to come from the same village. Aydin wept as his new friend shared the story of Jesus's crucifixion. He knelt in response. As far as is known, he was the seventh person from the newly independent country to become a follower of Jesus.

In the local culture, to believe is not a private thing: family and community must be told. He did so. His family's initial reaction was that he must have been taking drugs. Over time, they realized that something had changed and they liked the differences that they saw; many made the same decision to follow Jesus.

Persecution arose from a number of sources: family, society and the political system. He was arrested several times. The authorities had taken control of the KGB's local torture system for political prisoners and applied the same methods to religious opponents, including Aydin. He endured two weeks of intense "treatment" simply because he continued to speak about what he had seen and heard of Jesus (Acts 4:20) and to say that Jesus is the way, the truth and the life, and that nobody knows God as Father except through Jesus (John 14:6). The torturers told him never to speak about Jesus again.

Aydin felt obliged to leave the country. In Norway, he noted that even animals have rights, something that is denied to followers of Jesus in his country. Aydin had a childhood dream of being a KGB officer. One of his friends had the same dream and was able to pursue this in adulthood. Aydin's childhood friend was present at his arrest and witnessed him being tortured. The friend stood and watched as Aydin bled on the floor, and he urged Aydin to stop following Jesus. Ten years later this former friend contacted Aydin. The former childhood friends met in Istanbul. Aydin heard that his friend had lost his job, was impoverished and had several health issues. Aydin responded by offering his friend forgiveness for his part in his arrest, torture and forced exile from their country. He then offered him hospitality; the childhood friend and ex-torturer stayed with Aydin for three weeks. The friend remarked that he had been loyal to the secret police, but they had not been loyal to him. In contrast, he could see that Aydin's God had been faithful to Aydin. Consequently, the friend now wanted to follow the same God.

Aydin's warning is that the church must not lose its way in disorienting times. It must listen to Jesus as he shows us the way, so that it might show the world the way to the deep inner peace and sense of security found only in Christ. As Ramez remarked, the deepest longings of human beings find fulfilment only in Jesus. The cross, as Daniel noted, brings many benefits to Christ's followers.

Witness 2: Tahia – Choosing to Follow Jesus Cost Her Marriage

Tahia is ethnically Druze and holds Syrian nationality. For many years she sought a relationship with God through the religious rituals. This proved a disappointment: she could not find the relationship with God that she sought, so she continued her quest by exploring alternatives.

She moved to Lebanon where a relative introduced her to some Druze people who had become followers of Jesus. They were Christian in the religious sense of the term but retained their sense of being part of the Druze community.[23] She saw the relationship that these people had with God in prayer. Here was what she was seeking, but obtaining it for herself required a religious conversion. She was aware that this might be costly for her.

She returned home to Syria and began praying to God, asking to be shown which books to read. After twenty days she had a dream which she understood to be God telling her to read the Bible. There was a church in the town where she lived which she attended wearing typical Druze clothing. She began to participate in classes on spirituality which began by emphasizing the discipline of daily Bible reading, a practice often referred to as a "quiet time."

---

23. See Jonathan Andrews, *Identity Crisis: Religious Registration in the Middle East* (Malton: Gilead, 2016), 83–84.

As she had anticipated, conversion led to persecution. She was married with three children. Her husband forced her from their home and initiated divorce proceedings. This prompted Tahia to return to Lebanon where she was offered a job by a church. Her husband informed the children that their mother had died. Her eleven-year-old son had a dream in which his mother was described as having been reborn. He began visiting his mother on a regular basis. In contrast, seeing her daughter remains problematic. There is no law forbidding her from seeing her daughter. However, the divorce lawyer is asserting the ex-husband's control of the time and place of any meeting. He is understood to be concerned that his daughter might convert to Christianity. Tahia gave the lawyer a Bible and now asserts that Jesus is her lawyer and advocate. Her enduring hope is that she will meet her children in heaven.

For Tahia, the journey to and with Christ has proven costly.

Global Cross-Check: Victims or Heroes in the Search for Meaning? (by Gordon Showell-Rogers)

Following these witness statements, we move to take a global survey of religiously motivated persecution of Christians. This section has been provided by Gordon Showell-Rogers, a British citizen with many years' working experience in support of those persecuted for being or becoming Christians.

Suffering, evil and injustices in the world go on and on: epidemics, famine, sicknesses, human trafficking, global economic disparity, extreme climate events, water and food security issues, displaced people and refugees, wars and conflicts, and mass migration. Each of these contains untold numbers of personal tragedies, some of which see resolution and some of which do not. On top of all that, Christians face often severe persecution for their faith in Christ.

I would like to ask four questions that some might find provocative. First, have some of us glorified persecution for our own ends? Have stories been exaggerated, or told inaccurately, for less-than-honourable reasons? Second, do we sometimes elevate victimhood, defining the persecuted by the persecution instead of by their personhood or their identity in Christ? Does that glorify the perpetrator? Third, do those of us who lead comfortable lives sometimes bring "persecution" on ourselves because we are objectionable or because we are unwise in how we handle questions and criticism? Finally, why are many Western Christians so hesitant about sharing their faith?

There are often severe restrictions in the workplace in the West, but how many of us look for the "open windows" when a door closes? Ramez Atallah and his staff have set us an example. The reality is that the "restrictions" outside work are often social: so how will "embarrassment" stack up on judgment day as a reason for our not being open about our faith, when compared with torture or martyrdom? Having noted that, persecution for being Christian is a huge reality for many: it seems to be the Bible's expected "normal." It can be horribly painful, yet it is apparently also a way of knowing blessing, according to the New Testament (e.g. Matt 5:10; 1 Pet 1:6–9).

Let me give a few short illustrations of Christians in other contexts. In India the rise of Hindu nationalism is leading to religious persecution of Christians and others. In May 2014 the BJP party won an overall majority of the seats in the Indian parliament, allowing it to implement its right-wing, Hindu nationalist policy portfolio. One illustration of the growing pressure on Christians was the arrest on 21 May 2017 of seventy-one children and nine adults en route to a holiday camp. On 2 June, seven adults remained detained, having been charged with offences under state laws that restrict freedom of religion or belief.[24]

In Eritrea, with its Marxist ideology, there are multiple examples of pressure on evangelical Christians. Perhaps the best known are those held in container "prisons" where they experience extreme heat during the day and intense cold at night.

In Sri Lanka, with its Buddhist nationalism, there is an increasing number of attacks on Christians. Regular updates of such incidents are available from the Evangelical Alliance of Sri Lanka.[25]

Conflict appears endemic in parts of Nigeria. Yet, even in some such areas, Christians remain and continue to be the presence of Jesus.

Finally, returning to the West, there appear to be increasing occurrences in a variety of professions in the UK and elsewhere in Europe of Christians facing problems rooted in conscientious objection. One illustration is Swedish midwives objecting to involvement in abortions. Calls for "reasonable accommodation" appear to be falling on ever-less-responsive ears.

---

24. See, for example, Surinder Kaur, "Seven Christians Are Still in Custody after Christian Holiday Camp Arrests," Global Christian News, 2 June 2017, accessed 4 September 2017, www.globalchristiannews.org/article/seven-christians-are-still-in-custody-after-christian-holiday-camp-arrests/.

25. NCEASL, http://nceasl.org/, accessed 15 November 2017.

In Europe and other parts of the Western world, Christian understanding of life is too often shaped by a Christendom model of domination by one religion. I question whether that is, in essence, any different from the BJP's vision of Hindu nationalism, with all its implications for Christians and Muslims in India, or an Iranian or a Saudi Arabian model of public life. Meanwhile, on the other hand in Europe, the place of faith in public life is shaped by a post-enlightenment secularist model excluding people of faith conviction from public life, except – ironically – from those of the extreme secularist belief system.

As Os Guinness has argued, there is an alternative to the public square that is "sacred" (theistic) or "naked" (extreme secularist). Maybe churches should be prophetically offering that alternative: a "civic public square" based on the Global Charter of Conscience.[26] This was compiled in 2012 in response to a perceived marginalization of the right of freedom of conscience and in recognition of this right underpinning many other widely endorsed freedoms. In the words of Professor Heiner Bielefeldt, who was the UN Special Rapporteur on Freedom of Religion or Belief from 2010 to 2016, "secularity should provide an open, noisy and colourful space not an empty space."[27]

Maybe, in these times of disorientation, churches could, or even should, be at the forefront of those arguing the case for freedom of religion for all who do no harm, as found in the Universal Declaration of Human Rights (UDHR). Article 18 of that Declaration speaks specifically about "freedom of religion or belief" (FoRB), and two other Articles (19 and 20) are closely related. These Articles are about both internal issues – believing, not believing, changing religion, non-coercion – and external issues – association, expression, non-discrimination and state obligations to respect, protect and enable religious practices. Notice that the UDHR does not protect religions, but people. In other words, it does not advocate, for example, for "blasphemy laws." In these turbulent times, could one part of the prophetic role of churches be to be ambassadors of FoRB for all who do no harm? Our motivations include the fact that all people everywhere are made in the image of God and should therefore be treated with dignity, whatever religious convictions (or none) they hold. True worship must include freedom of choice.

---

26. See http://charterofconscience.org/, accessed 15 November 2017.

27. Included in comments during a UN Human Rights Council event, "Religions and Religious Freedom in International Diplomacy," 22–23 September 2016; summary available via www.ohchr.org/EN/Issues/FreedomReligion/Pages/InternationalDiplomacy.aspx, accessed 13 February 2018.

There is further food for thought in the story of the Good Samaritan – or the Good Neighbour – which tells us that the good neighbour is the one you do not like – and, in this story, the person of another religious persuasion (Luke 10:25–37).

Our theme is prophetic responses. So Micah may also have something to say to us in this context. Right after Micah 4:1–4, Micah 4:5 describes freedom of religion for all, in a world of peaceful co-existence in which the gospel is proclaimed. Our global prophetic response should arguably, therefore, include, first, defending the freedom of religion of all who do no harm; second, serving others' needs, irrespective of their faith or other differences; and third, contributing to community cohesion.

I finish with a reflection arising from the North Korean context. Dr Hyun Sook Foley and her husband work with North Korean defectors in South Korea. All the defectors' stories are initially defined by the single story of the dictatorial regime of North Korea. Dr Foley makes a compelling case for a "Hero's Journey" frame of reference, as advocated in Joseph Campbell's book *The Hero with a Thousand Faces*.[28] Dr Foley argues that we need to decide whether we want our stories to be "hero stories" or "victim stories." The difference between the two, she argues, is about whose story we connect our story to. She argues that if we tell our story as a victim story, it becomes that of the victimizer or perpetrator: for example, the story of Kim Il-sung, Kim Jong-il and Kim Jong-un. But if we tell the hero story that God tells about us, it becomes God's story. She points out that though it is not a story without suffering, it is a story with meaning and significance.[29]

An additional, related, insight is from logotherapy (see Glossary) which affirms the desire within human beings to find a sense of meaning and purpose, and the significant difference that makes to how they handle pain, disappointment and trials.

The question in all the pain of the world, for all those suffering for whatever reason, and perhaps especially for those being persecuted for being believers, may be as simple as this: Where is God in all this?

Maybe part of Jesus's answer to that question is his promise "to be with us" in the darkness. Maybe we first need to help one another to hear him say "see my hands and my side" (see Matt 28:20; John 20:27; Heb 13:5; and

---

28. Joseph Campbell's book *The Hero with a Thousand Faces* was first published in 1949 by Pantheon Books; further editions were published in 1968 and 2008.

29. Presentation at "Christian Women under Pressure for Their Faith" conference, Spring 2017, Belgium.

biographical or prophetic passages like Deut 31:6; Isa 43:1–2; Hag 1:13; Acts 18:10; and prayers like 1 Kgs 8:57). And maybe part of Jesus's answer is that he calls us to speak up – and even give our lives – for suffering humanity (see e.g. John 10:11; 21:22; 1 Pet 5:10; Rev 2:10).

Leading Prophetically

We have observed three types of persecution, namely religious, ethnic and national. The Israel–Palestine situation includes elements of all three, which is one reason for its profound complexity. Jewish and Christian Zionism is affecting Muslims and Christians as well as those we might term secular Jews. We will reflect further on this situation in chapter 3.

More generally, among the challenges faced by many is a sense of self-victimization, of perceiving oneself only as a victim. The counter to this is to keep one's story focused on what God is doing, not on what the perpetrator has done or continues to do. We described this as a sense of being a hero for responding appropriately. A deeper approach here arises from the search for meaning: the insight from psychology, logotherapy (see Glossary), that human beings become more resilient when they find a source of meaning and purpose. Jesus's followers can be very clear and assured that his presence with them fulfils their needs for identity, purpose and meaning whatever their circumstances.

We have observed a number of positive responses to suffering. A theology of suffering rooted in love, forgiveness and authentic witness is present in some parts of the MENA region. The expression of love towards persecutors needs to be relentless, and forgiveness needs to be clearly articulated (e.g. Matt 6:14–15; Eph 4:31–32; Col 3:13; Phlm 17–18).

Forgiveness is not appeasement; it acknowledges that wrong, injustice, has occurred. It invites the perpetrator to repent. It allows the offended to be generous to the extent that radical hospitality is displayed by some. It follows the example of Jesus who publicly forgave those who were torturing him to death on the cross, an unparalleled demonstration of moral strength (Luke 23:34).

It is not always clear how to seek justice. The balance between spirituality and activism, between contemplation and action, varies from person to person and place to place. So does the balance between direct proclamation of the gospel of Jesus and social action motivated by love of Jesus. Both are essential but finding the appropriate balance is context-specific. Some find very creative resistance motivated by love.

Many churches in the Middle East struggle with their relationship with the government. Should this be one of cooperation, of critique or of hiding? In changing times, what is appropriate and wise today might be different from what was possible in the past. Syria is one example, which we will explore further in chapter 3.

Similar considerations apply when reviewing relationships to Islam and Muslims. How do we respond to the violence of some which is equally appalling to many Muslims? In what sense is dialogue a way to witness? We will return to this question in chapter 4 and the appendix.

One tension that the Middle Eastern church continues to address is its understanding of its own theology. Many are critiquing aspects that have been imported, consciously or otherwise, from the West, some of which include colonialist attitudes and values. One example is Zionist theology, which is particularly poignant to Palestinians.

We have also seen the profound linkage between persecution and emigration, which we will explore further in the next chapter.

Questions for Reflection

1. What is the adequate/prophetic response to suffering that the Middle Eastern church should have?

2. What is the place of promoting freedom of religion and belief for all in our pursuit of justice? How can we articulate that such freedom includes conversion from and to all religions, including our own? Is this a prerequisite for the clear rule of law applied equally to everyone? Will our answers be the same in all contexts?

3. How can we avoid victim stories and consistently tell hero stories?

2

Emigration

In this chapter we address the issue of emigration and its impact on the local church and ministry. Our first contributor is Elie Haddad, who addresses voluntary emigration. He describes four reasons for emigration that he considers inappropriate and suggests how we might think differently about these issues. He is not arguing whether staying is good or bad, or whether staying is better than leaving. Rather, he argues that the reasons and motivations for staying or for leaving are very important. Proper decision-making is crucial. The future of the church and ministry in the MENA region is dependent on Christians being faithful to God's calling and sending.

This contribution is followed by Pastor Harout Seliman from Aleppo, Syria, who looks at emigration from a situation of overt, physical conflict. We follow this with brief Egyptian and Palestinian perspectives brought to us by Ramez Atallah and Daniel Bannoura, whom we met in chapter 1.

Our first witness account describes someone who returned to his native Lebanon thirty years after leaving for what he thought would be a short period abroad. Our second witness is an example of someone who left the region because of religious persecution and a cross-cultural marriage.

This chapter takes us on a five-country tour of the Middle East, starting in Lebanon.

Biblical and Theological Reflections on Emigration (by Elie Haddad)

People in the Middle East have always emigrated, mostly to the West, to seek a better future. This includes greater economic opportunities for those who have capital or who are willing to work hard for a better and more prosperous future, and highly educated people who can find significantly better career paths in the West. Christians in the Middle East, specifically, have also migrated for religio-political reasons.[1] Living in a majority Muslim context, in a highly sectarian region, many Christians seek to emigrate in order to secure a safer and more stable future for their families. Lebanon has had one of the highest emigration rates among Arab nations.[2] According to Akram Khater,[3] Lebanese have emigrated since the Ottoman Empire. He argues that the early emigration was motivated by economic reasons rather than by persecution of Christians.

In addition, wars and conflict have considerably contributed to emigration. This is referred to as forced migration whereby people are forced to leave their countries, or are internally displaced, due to extreme hardship such as war, conflict or natural disasters.[4] It is not my intention here to deal with the issue of forced migration. My objective is to think through voluntary emigration and its impact on church life and ministry in Lebanon and the region.

The rate of migration of church-attending people seems to match the trend within society at large.[5] This has led to a rapid decline in the attendance and ministries of our churches. Most of those who have means and are able to leave have done so. Those who have stayed are either those who had no opportunity to leave or those who have a high sense of calling to stay in spite of the strong temptation for a "better" life outside.

My own life story fits within this national trend. I emigrated from Lebanon at the age of thirty, lived in Canada for fifteen years, then felt called by God to return. My wife and I returned despite our negative feelings about Lebanon at that time. We had both emigrated independently because of the civil war in Lebanon and the declining economic opportunities. We did not leave as refugees; we do not fit the forced migration category. We left simply because we were presented with a better option.

When we received an invitation to come back to Lebanon, at a time when the migration trend was still flowing in the opposite direction, God convinced us of the need to move back and serve him in the community where we grew

---

1. See, for example, Jonathan Andrews, *Last Resort: Migration and the Middle East* (Malton: Gilead, 2017), 135–137.

2. "The World Factbook," CIA, accessed 11 May 2017, https://www.cia.gov/library/publications/the-world-factbook/.

3. Akram Fouad Khater, *Inventing Home: Emigration, Gender, and the Middle Class in Lebanon, 1870–1920* (Berkeley: University of California Press, 2001), EBSCOhost, http://search.ebscohost.com/login.aspx?direct=true&scope=site&db=nlebk&db=nlabk&AN=65886 (account required for access).

4. "Forced Migration Learning Module," Columbia University Mailman School of Public Health, accessed 11 May 2017, www.columbia.edu/itc/hs/pubhealth/modules/forcedMigration/definitions.html.

5. There is no hard data that confirms this observation.

up. God caused a major transformation in our thinking and our attitude to the extent that it became one of our priorities to work with young adults to help ignite a sense of purpose and a sense of calling to ministry in Lebanon, to give them reasons for staying rather than leaving. This topic for me is as practical and personal as it is theoretical.

When committed followers of Christ are faced with a decision of whether to stay or to leave, where do they go for direction? The Bible is the obvious first stop. However, the Bible is not that clear on this issue. In the mist of persecution and hardship, the New Testament church did not have a particular response. Some stayed and suffered, some were even martyred; others fled and scattered. God used people who stayed to show his glory through their perseverance and suffering. God also used those who fled to take the gospel to the diaspora.

Consider the apostle Paul: we find that many times he stayed, and suffered for his staying, and at other times he fled. It appears that it was frequently clear to him what God wanted him to do. The New Testament uses the language of "having been kept by the Holy Spirit from . . ." (Acts 16:6) as well as of "the Lord . . . has sent me" (Acts 9:17).

God sometimes instructs his people to stay and other times he sends them. Therefore, we cannot state that going or staying is right or wrong. The challenge must be in discerning where God is in the decision.

If the Bible is not clear on whether we should stay or leave, where else can we go for guidance? A wealth of literature has been written on migration, but mostly from the perspective of immigration: what happens at the receiving end. Not much is written, however, about emigration and the impact of leaving. Some secular literature discusses the social and economic impact of emigration.[6] In addition, there is some faith-based literature that addresses social issues as well.[7] But not much is written on the impact of emigration on the church and local ministry.

Martin Accad wrote an article on the theology of staying.[8] Martin presents four foundations for a theology of staying: trust in God, belief in the equal value of human beings, acceptance of the mysterious nature of evil and recognition of the all-embracing nature of sin. Martin's argument can be summarized by

---

6. The Center for Migration Studies has published several articles on the impact of emigration: http://cmsny.org, accessed 23 November 2017.

7. E.g. Michele R. Pistone and John J. Hoeffner, *Stepping Out of the Brain Drain: Applying Catholic Social Teaching in a New Era of Migration* (Lanham: Lexington Books, 2007).

8. Martin Accad, "When the State Starts Crumbling . . . A Theology of Staying," IMES blog, 20 March 2014, accessed 16 May 2017, https://imes.blog/2014/03/20/when-the-state-starts-crumbling-a-theology-of-staying/.

saying that bad circumstances do not justify leaving. We are not victims, as noted in chapter 1 and as will be discussed further in chapter 4. We may be part of the problem and can choose to be part of the solution.

Steven Cole wrote a Bible study on whether to move or to stay.[9] It is a biblical reflection on the story of Jacob. His conclusion is: "When considering a move, put God and his purposes first. That will bring everything else – your family, your ministry, your career – into perspective."

I do not want to argue that staying is right and leaving is wrong. However, we do need to recognize that, whether we decide to stay or to leave, our decision can be based on inappropriate motives. We tend to think, sometimes, that God is not concerned about the decisions we make as long as we remain "faithful" to him in the process. However, it is my contention here that our motivation for these life decisions is highly important to God.

In what follows I highlight what I regard as four inappropriate attitudes or reasons for leaving, and suggest what we can do to adjust our attitudes.

Inappropriate Attitudes 1: Compartmentalization

Compartmentalization of our lives is when we divide them into sections or parts. This is a common spiritual ailment. We recognize this phenomenon in theory, but it can be very hard to recognize, or admit, its manifestation in practice. We know, theoretically, that God is Lord over all aspects of our lives, yet the way we tend to make decisions is by trying to strike a balance between what we believe God wants and what we think is best for our families and the rest of life's demands. We have a tendency to think of priorities: God is first; family, second; work and ministry, third; and so on. This can be a dangerous way of thinking, balancing between God and family, and between ministry and safety and security.

I frequently observe symptoms of this among Christian leaders as they make decisions, putting security and safety for their families on a par with God's calling on their lives. I observe symptoms among some of ABTS's students. Some quickly identify what they are not willing to do after graduation and where they are not willing to go. Then they wait to hear God's calling. Unintentionally, they have drawn a clear boundary around where God is free

---

9. Steven J. Cole, "Lesson 77: Should I Move, Should I Stay? (Genesis 46:1–30)," Bible.org, accessed 16 May 2017, https://bible.org/seriespage/lesson-77-should-i-move-should-i-stay-genesis-461-30.

to call them. If God calls them outside this space, they think they are justified in not following or obeying.

Os Guinness defines calling this way: "Calling is the truth that God calls us to himself so decisively that everything we are, everything we do, and everything we have is invested with a special devotion, dynamism, and direction lived out as a response to his summons and service."[10] Guinness explains that God's calling us to himself is so decisive that it includes everything that we are, everything that we have, everything that is entrusted to us and everyone who is entrusted to us. This includes ourselves, our property, our time, our talents, our safety and security, our career, our education and our families. Guinness even uses the word "summons" as a synonym for God's calling. When God calls, there is only one valid answer: yes.

This understanding of God's calling means that the concept of priorities in our lives is wrong. There is only one priority: God. As Christians, we do not prioritize. We obey and follow.

When God calls, he knows our life circumstances, he knows our challenges, he knows our needs and those of our family. When he calls and we obey, we need to be assured of his provision for our needs and our family's needs. His provision does not guarantee an easy life or a safe and secure environment; but his provision is assured despite our circumstances and in the midst of them.

Bernard of Clairvaux brings us to the same conclusion in his treatise *On Loving God*.[11] Bernard talks about four degrees of love. The fourth and highest degree of love is "wherein man does not even love self save for God's sake." This means that we should not love anything or anyone in this world, not even ourselves, except for God's sake. We are faithful in our jobs for God's sake; we care for our families for God's sake; everything that we do should be for God's sake. We are not to split priorities between God and whatever else is in our lives: we do everything for God's sake. God's call, God's wishes, God's plans and God's purposes for our lives should be supreme, unimpeded and uncompromised. Anything less is spiritual adultery.

---

10. Os Guinness, *The Call: Finding and Fulfilling the Central Purpose of Your Life* (Nashville: W Publishing Group, 2003), 345.

11. Saint Bernard of Clairvaux, *On Loving God*, Project Gutenberg, 2007, accessed 23 November 2017, www.gutenberg.org/etext/21152.

Inappropriate Attitudes 2: God's Mission or Our Mission?

One of the most popular ideas about mission, ministry and work is that ministry and work are subjective: *our* ministry, *our* mission, *our* work. Surely our mission is to serve God! It follows that we can serve God wherever we are, whatever we do and no matter where we go. The need is everywhere. We get to decide where we serve and how we serve. We pray to God that he might bless our ministry or work; we take the initiative, and God ought to bless.

With this popular misunderstanding, we are free to decide whether to leave or to stay. We can serve God regardless of geography; so making a decision about leaving or staying is totally up to us. We evaluate our circumstances and make the best decision possible for us and for our families.

The last words of Jesus to his disciples before he ascended to heaven, his marching orders, were: "But you will receive power when the Holy Spirit comes on you; and you will be my witnesses in Jerusalem, and in all Judea and Samaria, and to the ends of the earth" (Acts 1:8). We conduct ourselves as if the power of the Holy Spirit is given to us as an additional weapon that we have in our arsenal or another trick in our bag of tricks. We get to decide whether we stay in Jerusalem or go to the ends of the earth, and we use the Holy Spirit to empower us along the way. The problem with this line of thinking is that the Holy Spirit is God. He does not come into our lives as a mere power subservient to our desires and wishes, no matter how "holy" we think they are. God comes into our lives only as Lord and master. He is the one to direct our lives, including our mission, our ministry, our work.

A document written by the Church of England asserts that "It is not the church of God that has a mission in the world, but the God of mission has a church in the world. . . . We join his mission. We should not ask him to join ours."[12] I agree with this declaration. We, as individuals, do not have a mission in the world, and we, as a church, do not have a mission in the world. It is the mission of God, *missio Dei*, the sending of God. His church, which includes all of us, ought to join his mission. This means that he is the one who sends. We obey and follow. He is the one who chooses whether we stay in Jerusalem or whether we go to the ends of the world. The power of the Holy Spirit is the power to guide and direct our lives under his lordship according to his sending. Anything less than that is spiritual adultery.

---

12. Paul Bayes and Church Army (Church of England), *Mission-Shaped Church: Building Missionary Values*, Grove Evangelism Series (Cambridge: Grove Books, 2004).

Inappropriate Attitudes 3: Open Doors / Closed Doors

In the parable of the sheep and the Good Shepherd, Jesus says that the sheep follow the shepherd because "they know his voice" (John 10:4). Nevertheless, the question most asked by believers is how to discern God's will in their lives. I find this perplexing. If we are expected to recognize his voice, why is it that frequently we do not? What is it that distracts us from hearing his voice? Our sinfulness must play a big role in it. Moreover, I suspect that our own desires and plans play a big role in it as well. Added to that, we do not have a proper framework for discerning God's will in the midst of our circumstances.

One of the problems is that we are inclined to discern God's will for our lives based on open doors and closed doors, or green lights and red lights. This type of thinking assumes that we are to enter every open door and stay away from every closed door. Conversely, this assumes that we are never called to persevere even in the face of closed doors, or to resist some open doors. I find this type of thinking very troubling, and the outcome damaging to the church.

During the various recent wars in our region, I have noticed how many church and ministry leaders were the first to pack up and emigrate, leaving behind the congregations that they were called to serve – and had faithfully served for a long time. It is the leaders who normally have the networks and connections and, therefore, have the option to leave. It is the leaders who have access to *open doors*, much more than the rest of their community. Should this always translate into leaders leaving because they encounter open doors, while their congregations stay and become shepherd-less because they face closed doors?

We need to find better ways for discerning God's will for our lives. Many good books have been written on this topic. Two of them particularly played a big role in my own life: Henry Blackaby's *Experiencing God*[13] and Dallas Willard's *Hearing God*.[14] There is nothing magical about discerning God's voice. The challenge is to be close to God, preferring his ways over mine, and his call over my comfort and safety. These books encourage us and guide us into becoming more spiritual in our daily lives so that we can be sensitive to God's voice.

Two quick principles from these books. First, according to Willard, once we are convinced what God's will for us is, we must do it "mercilessly." We do

---

13. Henry T. Blackaby and Claude V. King, *Experiencing God: Knowing and Doing the Will of God*, rev. ed. (Nashville: LifeWay Press, 1993).

14. Dallas Willard and Jan Johnson, *Hearing God: Developing a Conversational Relationship with God*, updated and expanded ed. (Downers Grove: IVP Books, 2012).

not question it, we do not rationalize or justify why we cannot do it; we just do it. As Ramez Atallah remarked in chapter 1, if we encounter a closed door, we must find a window to jump through. Second, according to Blackaby, if we are already doing what we know God has called us to do, we do not stop doing it until we clearly hear from God. If God put us in a certain ministry, we do not take ourselves out from it: only he does. If God places us in a certain location, church or community, we do not take ourselves away from it: only he does.

Inappropriate Attitudes 4: Imposing Our Worldview on the Bible

Suffering and pain have become so foreign to our Christian worldview that we tend to impose that understanding on our reading of the Bible. One popular example that I find is Acts 12, when Peter was delivered from prison. The way we read this passage is that Peter had been imprisoned and the church was praying for his deliverance. When he was delivered, he went to where the believers were gathered. He knocked on the door, but they hesitated to open the door because they did not expect him to be delivered. I have heard many conclude that the believers lacked faith. They were praying for his deliverance, but when he was delivered they did not believe. Actually, while the Bible tells us that they were praying for Peter, it does not mention what they were asking God to do for Peter. The passage does not explicitly state that they were praying for him to be delivered. I believe that the disciples expected to be imprisoned when preaching the gospel and they preached nevertheless: they were not afraid of prison nor deterred by it. I do not believe that Peter or the believers had any kind of expectation that he would be delivered from prison: imprisonment was the natural outcome of preaching the gospel. They were probably praying that God would strengthen him and use him in prison, but not necessarily deliver him. This is why they were surprised. God had at times allowed his disciples to be imprisoned and he was glorified through their imprisonment. At other times he delivered them from prison and was glorified through their deliverance. Our own expectation of being delivered from pain and suffering affects the way we read our Bible and, in turn, affects our decision-making regarding mission, ministry and work.

In his book *Shaped by the Word*, Robert Mulholland stresses that as we read the Bible, it should read us.[15] As we read the Bible, it exposes us: our attitudes, our understanding, our assumptions and our worldview. We do not

15. M. Robert Mulholland, *Shaped by the Word: The Power of Scripture in Spiritual Formation*, rev. ed. (Nashville: Upper Room Books, 2000).

manipulate the Bible by imposing our thinking on it; the Bible is the one that manipulates us by changing us and transforming us.

The previous chapter addressed the theme of pain, suffering and persecution. What we want to stress here is that we should not be influenced by our culture's worldview that encourages us to run away from any type of pain or suffering. Rather, we should be influenced by a biblical worldview and by what God wants to do in and through our lives.

The Challenge: Why We Stay or Why We Leave

The issue, therefore, is not in staying or leaving. The issue is in why we stay or why we leave. The church in our region has suffered a lot because many, especially leaders, have chosen to leave. The need in the MENA region is increasing: people from different faith backgrounds are open to hearing about Christ, while many in our churches are looking for safety, security and a better future. Hostilities in the region continue and the agents of reconciliation are departing. Despair abounds (as will be discussed in chapter 3) and the agents of hope are disappearing. It is God's design that his reign be manifested through kingdom citizens living out kingdom values. We are the ones blessed with the commission to declare God's identity in this precious region. To whom do we leave this task?

We should never judge those who leave or ridicule those who stay. God is free to call whomever he wishes to wherever he chooses. This is his mission field. However, is it not surprising that God seems to call non-Arabs to the difficult places in the Arab world (see Glossary) while he always calls Arabs to the West? Is it possible that we are not hearing God well? Is it possible that our own safety, security and prosperity are more important to us than God is? Is it possible that our worldview is superseding the Bible's?

Devotional Pause: Psalm 18 (by Gary Nelson)

> *Let us pause briefly before taking Syrian, Egyptian and Palestinian perspectives on emigration. This devotional pause looks at the stability that having a clear sense of God's call can bring in disorienting times.*

Psalm 18:1–19 is almost breathless in its pace. The writer, David, is experiencing God amidst the stress and distress of his situation. In the middle of chaos and danger his distress becomes raw emotion. He appreciates being alive and desires to remain so.

This is a psalm of thanksgiving written to keep hope alive in communities that were experiencing oppression. It is all about God, even though at first reading it may seem to be all about the psalmist. The focus is on God's sovereignty and his activity in the midst of difficult situations.

The flow of the psalm is wonderful. From an immediate burst of praise about who God is, the writer moves quickly to a description of his past circumstances. The drama unfolds. His situation was overwhelming but he cried out to God. The psalmist notes God's anger at what is happening to his people (18:7). Verses 7 to 17 contain colourful words which display God's righteous anger and indignation at the circumstances of his people.

Then it comes: the foundational reason for God's anger is that he delights in us (v. 19) – like a father whose delight in his children is transformed into righteous anger when those children are threatened or bullied.

This intimate declaration from the psalmist is a knowing response of one who has experienced this delight; one whose intimacy with God is such that his life is intricately woven together so that it is God's story in his story. Only that kind of intimacy can truly know when God is distant and far. Only that kind of intimacy cries out for God as lived experience and not simply an empty prayer. In times that are disorienting, as we noted near the end of chapter 1, we need to ask how God is at work in us, in the situations around us and through us, so that in difficult times we have a promise to cling to that grounds us.

A Syrian Perspective (by Harout Seliman)

The subject of emigration has been introduced to us by a Lebanese person whose life story includes emigration and subsequent return. We switch now to a Syrian perspective. Rev Harout Seliman lives and works in Aleppo. In his work, the subject of emigration arises daily, perhaps hourly. He is a church leader who has had opportunities to leave his city and country but has chosen to continue residing and working there.

Emigration is a much debated topic; and if anybody is an expert on this, it would certainly be a Lebanese! Yet during the last few years there has, to state the obvious, been an incredible increase in emigration from Syria. What follows is my [Pastor Harout's] perspective.

Acts 20:24 sums up my testimony at this time: "However, I consider my life worth nothing to me; my only aim is to finish the race and complete the task the Lord Jesus has given me – the task of testifying to the good news of God's grace." I hope I will not finish my life on earth soon, but I do feel that the situation in my country gives itself to thinking like the apostle Paul who "was on the move"; if you read any section from chapter 13 onwards of the Acts of the Apostles – I prefer to call it "The Acts of the Holy Spirit" – you will find Paul zigzagging through modern-day Turkey and Greece. There were riots, persecutions, times in prison and escapes, but what mattered to Paul was "finishing the race and completing the task the Lord Jesus had given him," which was sharing the gospel with as many people as possible in as many locations as possible. What an awesome task! So this is the goal set before us as followers of Jesus; and from Brother Elie's contribution it is obvious that this is his goal for himself and for those he engages with in his daily life as a communicator and Bible teacher.

So Where Are We Today?

In 2012, as conflict started in Aleppo, I received a phone call from a close friend who has known me since my teenage years. He asked: "How are you doing? Are you able to hang in there in Aleppo?" My reply then and ever since was: "Do you remember what our dear friend Brother Jack used to tell us? Syria is our country and we are staying!" This has gone through my mind often, knowing that many, many Christians in Syria have stayed on and have made their presence felt in our country. I think of them as saints.

One difference between Lebanon and Syria is that for many years Lebanon has had many foreign missionaries whilst Syria has had very few. But those missionaries who either have been with us or are still with us, mostly Catholic, have had a tremendous impact on the church in Syria. Wherever you go you find people who testify to their faithfulness and their love for Syria and its people. If you look at the Catholic Church you will find many nuns, also missionaries, including some from Lebanon, who have given much to the church in Syria; their lives have been a challenge to many. These people have challenged many to stay and be faithful in their various tasks. This is responding a little to the questions raised earlier in this chapter. Personally, I am not seeing or looking for the pastors, priests, leaders and church members who have left: I see only the ones who are still there, and I am both encouraged and impressed.

There is a challenge in the story of the wise men and Jesus and his family (Matt 2:1–18) – and it also makes me think of Elie's own "emigration and return." Matthew's Gospel contains many prophecies from the Old Testament being fulfilled, and this story is one of them since Matthew 2:15 quotes Hosea 11:1: "Out of Egypt I called my son."

Was the fulfilment of prophecies the "whole goal" of the family of Jesus going to Egypt? In this passage God guided the Magi, or wise men, from the east with a star going ahead of them. They had seen the star at the moment it appeared: God had been in this journey from the very beginning, and he would be with them until the end. However, the Magi made the mistake of thinking that the king must be born in a royal palace and for a moment they took their eyes off the "guiding star." As a preacher, I would say that the wise men had relied on their own wisdom and, without looking up at the star, logically went to the royal palace in Jerusalem to find the new-born king instead of following the star that had been going ahead of them. So the Magi, because of their disobedience and reliance on their own wisdom, brought not only the best and most valuable gifts to Jesus and his family; they also almost brought about the death of the Christ-child. They did actually bring about the deaths of many babies in Bethlehem. So what do we learn from this about the consequences of disobedience and the importance of obedience? As a result of this disobedience, God the Father stepped in by taking the whole family out of the danger zone.

Could not God have done something about King Herod? Could not God the Father have protected the Holy Family just where they were? I can see that many times we are so lost as human beings, even when we are close to God, that our heavenly Father takes us out of a situation just like this for our own security and safety and for a time of preparation. So should we encourage people to leave their countries for a while in order to become better prepared and equipped to serve there? We must admit that arriving in a new country these days does not seem to help in getting prepared for a return to the land of origin for a time of service there: few actually do come back.

Life and Christian Unity

There are two points for us to think about. The first one is the "normal one" that has to do with our mindset. When we talk about "our" ministry and "our" task in the church, what do we mean? Do we mean the things that we do inside the church, usually a building, or for the church? Or do we mean *life itself*? I have met many Christian leaders who talk about their "ministry" and ask me about my "ministry." Instead, I want to talk about life: *life* lived to the fullest and with a purpose, which we saw in that first verse quoted earlier from the Acts of the Holy Spirit. For me, *life* with Christ means exactly what various saints and writers from the past and today have been talking about: a life which is not only in a church and not only at home, but is in the church, at home, at school, at university and at work. To me there is no such thing as secular work. A baker, a barber, a banker, a driver, a farmer, a professor, a pastor, a Christian leader and anyone else: we are all the same. We are all one in Christ and together we are here to complete the task of testifying to the good news of God's grace – sometimes through words, both written and spoken. I believe that as a church we have for too long made too large a distinction between the spiritual world and the secular world, and this has made us into people who see only when the pastors leave and forget about the others who are still around doing the job.

The second topic that I need to raise is this. As a community leader, I deal with the many Christians and their leaders within the historic churches who are not evangelical. I cannot exclude them when I am talking about the church. For me, they are part of the one church that the apostle Paul wrote about – especially in the Middle East, where most churches are part of the historic denominations that trace their history back to the time of Christ's apostles. We must remind ourselves that they have carried the message of Christ since the time of Jesus. I have had the privilege of sitting at the feet of some true saints from these churches, and our conversations have been not about politics but about the risen Christ and his unchanging message. The Holy Spirit has been working in our lives and he has been working in their lives. We all need one another at this time when we so often need a shoulder to cry on.

So when we see people from our own churches emigrate we need the support and comfort of all the Christians of other church traditions as we continue living the faith in our own countries.

Trauma and Healing a Reason for Leaving?

When we "fight" against emigration, which most of us Syrians do at this time, I realize that in the church we have very little to offer to the people suffering. As one body, we suffer with them. But do we bring healing? Is there a mechanism in the church of today to handle victims of trauma? I might have one person in my church able to treat a trauma victim, but the needs are terrific. All that has happened has come so fast; how could anybody be prepared for such an onslaught of suffering and needs?

Visiting people who fled from Kessab for the third time in little more than a century helped me to understand a little about the effects of trauma. Most people survived the onslaught but many died once they came back home again. The trauma of forced evacuation is something of which few of us know the depths and limits.

I am aware of an Iraqi priest who has been dealing with the effects on nuns in the aftermath of the events on the Nineveh Plain (see Glossary) in 2014. This priest says that eighteen nuns subsequently died, almost all of whom had been living in shock and were in great need of counselling. This has of course deeply affected the "normal" displaced people as they had come to rely on the encouragement of the church to keep on living under very challenging circumstances. The fact is that some of the most effective counsellors and members of the Christian community have suffered so much that they have had to step aside, too wounded themselves to assist others.

Here we have seen the trauma affecting people immediately after the tragic events, but in some cases the trauma victim does not admit or experience the distressing and disorienting results of trauma until years later. When people come to me and I can tell from the beginning that these people need to be treated, I realize that as a church we are up against a wall. If they leave us and their home country there is a greater opportunity for them to be treated than in our own community, which is very judgemental when it comes to people "having gone mad," as we call it. Such people need another situation, which our country cannot provide at this time. Some of these trauma victims are religious leaders and church leaders. When hearing about the increase in medication that people across Syria have been taking since 2011 I realize that there are so many things that make people lose both their minds and their health. Could we dare to say that the war is behind so many people suffering from high blood pressure and diabetes?

A friend of mine, a pastor who is much older than me, said about war and living in war: "When your wife cannot take it any more, it is time that you left." When you see people suffering mentally and physically due to sieges, shelling, kidnapping, killing and the severing of heads, what message do we dare give to our members?

Job Opportunities, Family and Finance: Causes of Pressure

In my own community there are few, if any, people in government employment; like so many Armenians in other countries they have their own shops, garages and other personal enterprises. Massive emigration, displacement and conflict have put an end to much trade to the extent that many people who were once well-off can no longer make ends meet. Some have been more or less unemployed for five years. The reunification of the city of Aleppo during 2017 had not by summer 2017 improved the situation enough to give people much hope for the future. If they had had a government job with a steady income, things would have been much easier. I look at these church members and say to myself: "These people are really living by faith on a daily basis. They really do need to pray: 'Give us today our daily bread.'"

How easy do you think it is for the family whose house was not destroyed and whose relatives, displaced by the war, have come to live with them? I look at these families that used to want to be together every day of the week and see how they, by now, have had enough of living together, sharing everything and always thinking about the future and what they should do. If you want to see challenges to people's marriages, come with me and visit some of these families and observe how they retreat into "their corner" of the house if it is large enough. Problems in earning an income make matters worse, intensifying the situation for all involved. I have got the right Bible verses for all situations, but seeing what is really happening makes me helpless and, I regret to say, feel totally useless.

This forces me to bring up another sensitive issue. Most pastors or Christian leaders are community leaders and provide guidance and advice through their own exemplary living right in the midst of society. All eyes are on them and on what they do and what they do not do. These leaders must be able to come up with the right thoughts at all times, especially when it comes to trusting God, and we certainly share them with our church members as often as we can. We read these beautiful verses, which I certainly believe in with all my heart: "Therefore I tell you, do not worry about your life, what you will eat or drink; or about your body, what you will wear. Is not life more than food, and the body more than clothes? Look at the birds of the air; they do not sow or reap or store away in barns, and yet your heavenly Father feeds them. Are you not much more valuable than they?" (Matt 6:25–26).

Who does not love those verses? And then we continue reading: "So do not worry, saying, 'What shall we eat?' or 'What shall we drink?' or 'What shall we wear?' For the pagans run after all these things, and your heavenly Father knows that you need them. But seek first his kingdom and his righteousness, and all these things will be given to you as well. Therefore do not worry about tomorrow, for tomorrow will worry about itself. Each day has enough trouble of its own" (Matt 6:31–34).

If you are like me, you read these verses to yourself over and over, especially at a time of need such as we face in Aleppo at present. In these circumstances I read them to make them part of my own life so filled with reasons to worry and be concerned. I wish I could tell you that I do not worry, but I do. Yet many times I do not worry because of danger, but because of lack of money to take care of myself and my family. We are well aware that some of my colleagues choose either to stay as pastors for ever, until ninety years of age in some cases, or to emigrate to a country at the age of fifty or fifty-five so that they can pastor a church for a while and end up with a pension. Is this not the truth?

There are not many graves of evangelical pastors in our countries. A large number moved on at an early age to secure "some kind of future" for themselves and their families. We can criticize them, but have we done enough to make them feel appreciated and secure where they have been serving faithfully for years and years? This is not "forced" emigration, but how much of a burden of sacrifice should we place on pastors and Christian leaders? I have the same concern for "normal" Christians, which we should all be.

The Challenge Continued

Are there areas of disagreement or contention with the above? I appreciate that it challenges our problem of emphasizing priorities when our only concern should be God. The Bible challenges us and this brings contention to our hearts.

I have heard people say that church leaders in Lebanon only spoke against emigration to keep "their numbers up," but did not do anything to help the people once they stayed on. They were left in poverty and struggle daily to survive. I think Elie's contribution is directed more to church leaders than to "normal" Christians. The change must happen in the lives of the leaders and they must in practical ways look after the needs and aspirations of the people within the church. All Christians should have the same access to open doors.

How might we encourage faithfulness to Christ within the midst of these challenges? The leadership must be totally faithful to Christ. We must live Christ at all times; there is no other way. It means following his commandments, and the greatest of these is to love one another and all others. When we as leaders do this, I believe that incredible things will happen in the church.

What opportunities do these situations provide to the church in terms of its ongoing witness in the region? As a church we have had so many opportunities to witness in our city of Aleppo, which we have never had before. Around the Armenian Christmas we as a church decided to invite all the street sweepers (garbage collectors) in the city for a Christmas party. We also invited the heads of Aleppo municipality. What an afternoon we spent together, taking down the barriers between the high and the low: this was truly a Christian witness showing that Jesus Christ has come to all and for all.

What has the church been learning about itself and its role in society through these times? The church has learned that it has got an amazing place in the community, especially in a country like Syria. You might think that the church is insignificant in the big political struggle between nations, but on a local level nobody counts its size when it starts acting as the body of Christ.

The main need initially was food aid, which was distributed without discrimination. In 2017 we started micro-enterprise projects to contribute to creating a long-term future: new small businesses as an essential element in improving the local economy. In such ways the church has been doing things that neither the government nor the municipality has been able to do. When hospitals had to close down we opened a dispensary for people from all backgrounds. When schools have closed, we kept our schools running, with excellent results. When there has been no help forthcoming from other sources, the church has opened its doors to give. We have certainly learned that numbers do not count; rather it is the willingness to be and to give that matters.

How do we, as the body of Christ, discern God's will for the church and its members in the face of such adversity? What does it mean to be a prophetic community?

Is it presumptuous to say that we knew it all along? But it really is all there in the Bible, as Brother Elie has pointed out. Jesus told us to be there; he gave us a message; he told us that he would be there with us. He has conquered the world, and so have we.

An Egyptian Perspective (by Ramez Atallah)

We will look at this issue from an Egyptian perspective provided by Ramez Atallah, whom we met in chapter 1.

Thousands of Christians emigrate from Egypt annually seeking the "better life." Many of these are Christian leaders and some are pastors. In most cases they are encouraged to do so by their family, friends and churches. Some claim that they are following God's call – even though it is surprisingly always to a Western country rather than to a developing, needy state. The more honest ones acknowledge that getting a visa to a Western country is "an opportunity" which they cannot resist. I have yet to meet a person who was an active Christian leader in Egypt who would claim to be more actively involved in Christian ministry in his or her new home in the West than he or she was back home.

Some people have accused me of not being sensitive enough to people's needs and aspirations, and of condemning those who emigrate as not being committed enough to remain in a difficult situation. This is a complete misunderstanding of my stance. What I firmly believe is that many, though not all, of those who emigrate to the West have a harder time as believers than they would have had if they had stayed in Egypt. They emigrate hoping to have an easier life for themselves and their children and more freedom as Christians. Yet they rarely find this dream accomplished in the long term. Many Middle Eastern Christians are ignorant of the difficulties they are likely to encounter should they move to the West, some of which were described in chapter 1.

This reflects the deeply ingrained belief among many Christians that it is a foregone conclusion that one should choose the path in life which will give me and my family the greatest degree of comfort, safety and security. This, of course, is what most people on the planet seek. This perception is rightly challenged by Elie Haddad's contribution: it is not what Jesus expects of his followers.

The main exception to this is for Muslim converts whose life in Egypt is often extremely difficult. For some, emigration is the only viable option, as we saw for Aydin and Tahia in chapter 1 and others whose situation will be described later in this chapter.

A Palestinian Perspective (by Daniel Bannoura)

Palestine has been profoundly affected by emigration for decades. It is one possible response to the multi-layered suffering being endured by the population, Muslims as well as Christians, that Daniel Bannoura described in chapter 1. From many perspectives, the situation appears bleak: consequently, some emigrate. Daniel now adds this contribution to what he presented in chapter 1.

In 2017 it was estimated that there were 160,000 to 165,000 Palestinian Christians, of whom 120,000 lived in Israel and 40,000 to 45,000 in the West Bank and the Gaza Strip. Christians are between 1 and 2 percent of the population. In contrast, we were 12 percent in 1967. It has been a story of constant decline since that time.

One dynamic within the Christian communities concerns those resident in the Gaza Strip. Many who visit the West Bank at Christmas and Easter do not return home. Consequently, the Christian communities across the Gaza Strip are declining.

The Christian community consistently urges people to be wise, prophetic and patient. We need to have a sense of hope even when we cannot see anything likely to bring positive change to the context in which we live. This will be explored further in the following chapter. We need to be faithful witnesses to Christ, and bring this much-needed hope to our society. We are also consistently clear that we are not going anywhere: we are Palestinians and we will remain in our communities.

Churches of all traditions and denominations working together is something that strengthens us all by enhancing our calls for justice. The Kairos Document is one example of this. If I am honest, the tradition within Christianity that is typically perceived as the hardest for others to work with in my context is my tradition, the evangelical tradition. Zionist theology-type thinking within parts of this tradition is one factor in this.

We move from a national overview perspective to look at the stories of two families, both of which have migrated more than once.

Witness 1: Kamel's Temporary Move Abroad Lasted Thirty Years

Kamel Shalhoub grew up in Tripoli, northern Lebanon. His Christian faith was always a significant part of his life. On leaving school, his desire was to study engineering at the American University of Beirut (AUB). Alas, he was not offered a place there because nobody he knew had the *wasta* ("influence"; see Glossary) needed at that time. He was, though, offered a place at an American university and the necessary student visa for the USA.

He enjoyed his time at university, except for the quietness of the campus during the vacations when only the expatriate students were resident. During one vacation Kamel's attention was drawn to Acts 13:47, which refers to witnessing to Gentiles.[16] He sensed God saying that he would one day be working among Muslims in his own country. Little did he know how long this call of God would take to be fulfilled.

---

16. "For this is what the Lord has commanded us: 'I have made you a light for the Gentiles, that you may bring salvation to the ends of the earth'" (Acts 13:47, quoting Isa 49:6).

He graduated and was offered a job in engineering in California. His intention was to work for two years and then return to Lebanon. Two events occurred which changed his plans. First, he met and married Badia, who is also Lebanese. Second, their first child, a daughter, was born and quickly diagnosed as being deaf. "Why, Lord?" Kamel asked his God. "Why not?" was what he heard in reply.

The year was 1977 and Badia and Kamel were reliably informed that there was very little, if any, provision of education for deaf children in Lebanon at that time. For the sake of their child, they decided to remain in the USA where the educational provision was excellent. Their second child was also born deaf.

Kamel experienced many years of brokenness before God over why his daughters were born deaf and the effect this had on fulfilling what he sensed was his calling of returning to Lebanon and being involved in Christian work. Badia was very steadfast throughout these years. Verses such as Ezekiel's "the hand of the LORD was on him" and similar sustained them (e.g. Ezek 1:3). Kamel's desire to share the good news of Jesus remained strong, and during this period it was fulfilled among local communities and by giving financially to those able to be involved abroad. The years passed and their daughters grew up.

One day, Kamel and Badia were approached by Navigators, a Christian organization. Would they be willing to return to Lebanon and take the position of leader for their work in the MENA region? Their daughters were now adults; one was married and they now had a grandchild.

The Navigators' request challenged their sense of being comfortable in their situation. Kamel remembered the verse from Acts that had attracted his attention thirty years previously. The couple made the move, accepting all that it involved for them and their family.

Five principles guided their thinking then and indeed still in their continuing work in Lebanon. They are rooted in the injunction in Matthew 6:33 to "seek first" God's kingdom: (1) to maintain a daily walk with God, pressing always to know him more and listening attentively to the Holy Spirit; (2) to seek the call of God in our lives, both generally the call to know God himself and the specific call to do something; (3) to seek intimacy with Christ, and keep alert to ways to fulfil the Great Commission of making disciples of all nations (Matt 28:17–20); (4) to seek the counsel of godly Christians who know us well, since guidance on specific decisions usually involves corporate as well as individual dimensions; and (5) to know the peace of God that is not based on circumstances.

Kamel visited Rev Lucien Accad when his friend was close to death. Lucien asked why so many Christians were leaving and who would do the ministry. Kamel took this as an injunction to ask all Middle Eastern Christians to be attentive to the call of God. This is the same message as given above by Elie Haddad.

Witness 2: Ash's Journey to the USA via Lebanon

Ash is from a Middle Eastern country. His story illustrates the challenges faced by those who choose to emigrate and the reasons why some are obliged to accept them.

Ash was born into a Muslim family. He converted to Christianity when he was eighteen. He continued living with his parents while he completed his studies and then got an office-based job. He attended a church when he could and maintained his Christian faith. When he was twenty-seven he moved to Lebanon and began studying theology. Why did he make this decision?

Living with his parents was fine for some of the nine years from his conversion to emigration. At other times it was difficult, with harassment including occasional assaults: he lived in fear of when his parents would inflict the next attack. The decision to leave his country was not made easily: it meant leaving his friends as well as his family. He travelled by land, pausing at the border to look back and wonder when, if ever, he might see his parents and his home country again.

For Ash, life in Lebanon was very different. He was now living in a communal and multi-cultural setting at ABTS and studying theology rather than working. The study did not come easily to him. It is often the case that theological study is subtly disorienting: good lecturers will always challenge students to think why they believe what they do and to explore alternative perspectives before arriving at a settled, richer and fuller understanding of the God they love, worship and follow.

In Lebanon, some Christians urged Ash to explore leaving the region. They proposed that he approach the embassies of various Western countries to enquire about obtaining a visa. Ash did not sense God's call in this and steadfastly resisted such pressure. He quietly completed his course and started working for a Christian organization. He established some good friendships and came to feel that he belonged.

Another major event occurred in Ash's life in Lebanon: he met an American lady who was a student at the AUB. They married in Lebanon, a country that they viewed as a half-way house between their two countries of birth. His wife was resident in Lebanon on a student visa. As she approached her graduation the couple were faced with a decision: they needed to establish settled residency somewhere. They decided to move to the USA, which for his wife meant returning home and for Ash meant a second emigration. Ash found unpacking the boxes of possessions very difficult, a not-uncommon experience for those whose cross-national marriage has necessitated a move.

Ash and his family arrived in the USA in 2012. The context was difficult, with much suspicion from local people about someone from the Middle East, a region with several conflicts and much political instability following the eruption of the Arab Spring the previous year. On occasions he was fearful of walking in the street.

As with his previous move to Lebanon, in the USA he had a new place to live, new work and he had no roots established during his childhood and adolescence. He understood much of the language but not the jokes. He felt lonely, despite the support of his wife and her parents.

Looking back, he realizes that he had some stability in his home country but also much instability. He felt forced to leave and identifies easily with the forcibly displaced and those labelled "refugees." The relationship with his parents has improved over time, for which he is profoundly thankful. Ash recognizes that returning to his country of birth would be fraught with difficulty and danger, potentially for others as well as for himself. He appreciated being able to visit Lebanon to attend the conference in June 2017 and would like to return on a longer-term basis at some point. For the present, he endeavours to be content with living in the USA and working among fellow immigrants from the Middle East whether they are Christian or Muslim. He, together with his wife, is attentive to the call of God.

Global Cross-Check: Canada – A Nation of Immigrants (by Greg Butt)

Greg Butt is Canadian and is the pastor of a church in Calgary. This is the third church that he has led during twenty-five years in church leadership. He is married, has six grown children and two grandchildren. Greg spent twelve years in India where his parents were missionaries and had travelled to forty countries by the time he was fifteen. Greg looks at emigration from the perspective of a country known for receiving immigrants, both as refugees being resettled and those moving by choice. This section describes the role of churches in welcoming and receiving immigrants. It examines the biblical mandate for radical hospitality.

In many ways I feel as if I know nothing about the depths of Christianity coming from the adversity experienced in the Christian church in the Middle East. I have, though, felt what it is like to be a minority, and on a minor scale have felt what it is like to be beaten for my faith – somewhat ironically, in a missionary boarding school.

Immigration has been a central theme for my country since its inception in 1867. Most people resident in western Canada are within 100 years of an immigrant family. With the physical space of one of the largest countries in the world, we have room to grow numerically.

Canadian culture has some strengths as well as real weaknesses. There can be a facade of people not talking to one another due to many working long hours, giving little time for community. There are some clashes within close communities. In general, Muslims are welcome even if they are not widely understood. The education system teaches all to get along with others, including those who are different.

The annual number of immigrants to Canada has fluctuated considerably over the last 150 years. For example, in the late 1800s the number admitted annually varied between 6,300 and 133,000. Record numbers were admitted in the early 1900s when the government was promoting settlement in western Canada. The highest number ever recorded was in 1913, when more than 400,000 people arrived. However, the number of people entering the country dropped dramatically during the First World War, to fewer than 34,000 during 1915. The lowest numbers were recorded during the Great Depression in the 1930s and during the Second World War. The end of that conflict fostered economic recovery and an immigration boom. Other record levels of immigration were registered during political and humanitarian crises, including in 1956 and 1957 when 37,500 Hungarian refugees arrived, and in the 1970s and 1980s when a large number of Ugandan, Chilean, Vietnamese, Cambodian and Laotian refugees were admitted. Since the early 1990s, the number of immigrants has remained relatively high with an average of approximately 235,000 per year. It is important to note that of the 300,000 coming to 350 Canadian communities in 2016, only 47,600 fell under the status of refugees and humanitarian visas. Of these, about 25,000 were Syrian refugees; we have received approximately 40,000 Syrian refugees since the conflict in Syria began in 2011. By far the majority of immigrants are migrating by choice rather than by being displaced.

As a result of this constant theme of immigration, Canada is quickly becoming extremely diverse. Toronto has been officially named by the BBC as the most diverse city in the world with over 230 nationalities represented there.[17] Most churches I know host several ethnic congregations with varying degrees of integration – from providing a rental of the building but no joint activities, all the way to full amalgamation. For example, in my mother's church they began renting to a Filipino congregation several years ago and by 2017 had fully integrated to the point of changing the name of the church to reflect the character of that diversity. In my church, we rent to a South Indian Orthodox church, a Korean Presbyterian church and a Filipino independent church. None of these groups would have been present in Calgary in large numbers in the 1980s. We are exploring various partnership options with these groups but as of mid-2017 had come together for only three or four joint services a year. I have expressed to all congregations that we need to be working together more deeply, for two reasons. First, in heaven we will all be together, so we probably should start now. Second, in ten years the children in all these groups will feel Canadian and start to pull away from fully identifying with their country of origin. Therefore, we should help the children worship together, as part of a broader, diverse community.

I have personally had exposure to six immigrant families. Two of these are evangelical Christian families from Aleppo. The others are a Catholic family from Damascus, a nominal Christian family from Aleppo, a Muslim family from Damascus and a single man from Eritrea joining his family in Calgary. Most of these families are coming to Calgary either directly or indirectly because of war or persecution. They all hope that things will be better financially, but that is not their prime motivation. Although they all prefer and love their country of origin, they have lost hope that they can go back in the short term. In all my years I have heard of only one person who has chosen to go back to the country of origin because of not liking Canada.

Pastor Mouner is from Aleppo. He says that, while some aspects of Canada are freer for Christians, he actually finds ministry harder. Whereas in Aleppo his ministry was primarily to Muslims and sharing Christ's love, in Canada it has been much more about trying to help lukewarm Christians regard their religious beliefs and practices as fundamental to their sense of identity (this is similar to what Ramez Atallah noted earlier).

When I look at the Scriptures, I find that there is much that speaks to these issues for us. Of particular challenge to us is what it means to be hospitable, especially as it pertains to strangers and foreigners in our land. As Christians,

---

17. "BBC Names Toronto the Most Multicultural City in the World," Notable Life, 16 May 2016, accessed 7 November 2017, http://notablelife.com/bbc-names-toronto-the-most-multicultural-city-in-the-world/.

we believe we are all foreigners in this world. This world is not our permanent residence (e.g. Heb 11:13; 13:14). So we need to hold the place where we have been put lightly. When you examine the Greek and Hebrew roots of helping the stranger among us, we are quickly led to the central theme of the Scriptures: to love God and our neighbours with all our soul, mind and strength (Mark 12:30–31; Luke 10:27).

This leads us to hospitality. Hospitality opens the door to uncommon community. It is no accident that "hospitality" and "hospital" come from the same Latin word, for they both lead to the same result: healing. In the Old Testament, showing hospitality was a cultural norm. The New Testament frequently encourages us to practise hospitality and to offer hospitality without grumbling (e.g. 1 Pet 4:9). In English, we typically understand hospitality as a willingness to host, feed and entertain a guest, something we all do, especially with our friends. However, the biblical term has a much deeper and more difficult meaning. The Greek term that is often translated into the English term "hospitality" is the word φιλόξενος: φιλό (*philo*) means "brotherly love" or "to love like a brother," and ξενος (*xenos*) means "stranger" or "immigrant." In light of these two words being combined, "hospitality," as commonly understood, is not exactly the best way to express this biblical truth. Instead of simply "entertaining guests" the word becomes "loving strangers/immigrants as you would your own brother." In Romans 13 we are told to "practise hospitality," that is, to go out of your way to do so: loving strangers and immigrants as if they were our siblings. This would mean that we do not withdraw from immigrants, legal or undocumented: that we do not allow them to go homeless or hungry and that we actually practise going out of our way to take care of them. It means that, when we are faced with immigrants and strangers in our churches, we do not create separate ministries for them in order to be able to keep our distance from them.

It goes even deeper: within the semantic range and historical uses of ξενος (*xenos*) we find that it did not simply mean "stranger" or "immigrant." This word has a dual usage that includes "enemy," since some cultures used the same word to refer to both groups. In addition, "strangers" were often seen or assumed to be enemies. So, in this case, the word "hospitality" becomes "loving your enemies in the same way that you love your brother." Grasping the depths of the flavour of ξενος, we see the New Testament epistles reaffirming the teachings of Jesus in regards to loving our enemies, especially in refraining from violence towards our enemies. Which one of us would let our brother go hungry? Which one of us would let our brother go homeless? Which one of us would be willing to kill our brother for any reason? Probably not many, I hope.

Both Jesus and Paul say that this is the way we are to love our enemies: in the exact same way that we would love our own brother or sister. Blessing instead of cursing; love instead of hate. It is beautiful. Radical. This is hospitality.

We need to ask ourselves: Can an immigrant become a leader in our churches? Can a Syrian pastor a Lebanese church? Can a white Caucasian be pastored by a man of colour? When people show up at our doors, is there any distinction between the hospitality we show our wealthy guests and that which we show our poorer guests? Do we put the same effort into training the refugee Christian for ministry as we do North Americans?

I hope we can consider the ways in which we do, or perhaps do not, show brotherly love to immigrants, strangers and enemies. In chapter 1, Aydin gave us an example of hospitality towards a friend who became an enemy before returning to being a friend. We must remember: whether they are immigrants, strangers or enemies who want to destroy us, these are human beings with unsurpassed worth, so valuable that Jesus gave his life for them. In fact, they may even be Jesus to us. Our job is simply to affirm their worth and love them like family.

Leading Prophetically: Being Faithful to the Call of God

A recurring theme through this chapter is the call of God. Primarily this is God calling us to himself, to be his children. Second, the discernment of God's call to specific tasks or decisions involves collective as well as individual guidance: we are not Christians in isolation but part of his one church. In disorienting times, we need one another. Once identified and agreed with others, our calling must then be pursued with determination. Some obstacles are there to be overcome, to be worked around. The simplistic criterion of what options are easily available should not be overly influential in our decision-making.

We have heard a passionate plea from a Lebanese Christian leader encouraging fellow leaders throughout the region to stay wherever possible. In addition, we heard a Syrian pastor call for effective support of such people in ways that respect and honour the local agenda.

We have observed several situations where for Christians to leave can be viewed as the only viable option. This applies to some, but not all, Christians in Syria. It applies to a few of Christ's followers from Muslim backgrounds.

We examined and challenged several all-too-common misconceptions. We need to remain faithful to our calling.

We looked at the biblical mandate for radical hospitality, one that treats those that the world would describe as enemies in the same way that we would treat a sibling. The church truly should be the family of God's people.

We are aware that there is (at the time of writing) conflict and strife in parts of the Middle East. For some, this produces a sense of hopelessness and despair. How can the church be the presence of Jesus to such people? This is the focus of the next chapter. If hopelessness and despair is one reason why some desire to emigrate, how can the church change their context so that they want to stay? This is one motivation for seeking to bring hope. It is, though, by no means our only reason.

Questions for Reflection

1. How does the temptation of Christian leaders to leave the region fit into the very evident move of God across the region? Why are they swimming against the tide?

2. How can we protect ourselves, individually and collectively, from four inappropriate attitudes: compartmental thinking, presuming that we own God's mission, open/closed door thinking and misreading Scripture?

3. How can we be more attentive to God's voice and to hearing his call for us, individually and collectively?

3

Hopelessness and Despair

This chapter takes us on a tour of the Middle East, visiting, in order, Israel–Palestine, Syria, Egypt and Lebanon. The collective cry we hear is that Christians should be, and in many locations are, at the forefront of community efforts to bring hope and transformation to situations that others regard as hopeless. This does not come easily and only rarely does it happen quickly. The process includes the recognition of deep pain as a necessary prelude to working for transformation. The theme of challenging injustice recurs.

One observation that will assist us concerns imagination. Linguistically, the opposite of hope is despair. In practice, hopelessness and despair are characterized by a lack of imagination. Part of restoring hope is to enable imagination since this brings awareness that lives and situations can change, that transformation is possible. Can we say that the opposite of hope is a lack of imagination? Maybe not linguistically, but in practical action it gives us a tool for identifying hopelessness and a starting point for bringing hope.

A Theology of Tears: Cry with Us (by Yohanna Katanacho)

We begin with a contribution by Yohanna Katanacho who lives and works in Nazareth. Ethnically, he is Arab and Palestinian; his nationality is Israeli. He works at the Nazareth Evangelical College. His reflections are rooted in an intense, passionate and insightful engagement with the Bible applied to the situation of his people.

This section presents a theology of hope in the midst of tears. It focuses on the book of Lamentations, which highlights the different human responses to a theo-political catastrophe, the fall of Jerusalem in 587 BC and consequent exile of many Israelites to Babylon. There was no comforter, no prophet and no hope. We will observe significant correspondences with Palestinian and other Middle Eastern catastrophic realities of the twenty-first century. These offer us important lessons that Christians need to consider in their prophetic imagination.

During the last few years, and in light of the realities in the Middle East, I have been studying the book of Lamentations. The similarities of pain shocked me and I was moved to write the following poem:

Cry with Us

This is a season of weeping and mourning,
but it is not void of hope.

Our tears are the bridge between brutality and humanity.

Our tears are the salty gates for seeing a different reality.

Our tears are facing soulless nations
and a parched mentality.

Our tears are the dam preventing rivers of animosity.

For the sake of the mourning men,
cry with us to reflect your amity.

For the sake of the poor children,
cry with us demanding sanity.

For the sake of lamenting mothers,
refuse violence and stupidity.

Love your enemies and cry with them
is the advice of divinity.

Blessing those who curse is the path to genuine spirituality.

Pouring tears of mercy and compassion is true piety.

Pray with tears, for the sake of spreading equity.

Followers of Jesus: crying is now our responsibility.

But do not cry for your friends only;
but also for your Enemy.[1]

I had many existential questions: What do we say or do when our cities collapse and hunger invades our streets? How do we respond when homes are destroyed and young children are brutally killed? What do we do when

---

1. Yohanna Katanacho, *Praying Through the Psalms* (Carlisle, UK: Langham Global Library, 2018), vii.

the teeth of evil are like nails from hell penetrating our souls? Why is God seemingly absent when the civic and moral infrastructure of our society collapses? Why does God appear to forsake us when our holy places are defiled and our religious symbols are despised? The book of Lamentations hosted my feelings and helped me to express my frustrations. It says:

> Streams of tears flow from my eyes
> because my people are destroyed.
> My eyes will flow unceasingly,
> without relief,
> until the LORD looks down
> from heaven and sees.
> What I see brings grief to my soul
> because of all the women of my city.
>
> (Lam 3:48–51)

Many other contemporary scholars have had a similar experience with the book of Lamentations during harsh times.[2]

There is no doubt that Lamentations is full of sorrow, sadness and salty tears. In the Septuagint (see Glossary) and Latin versions the book starts with an introduction that names Jeremiah as its author. In the Syriac version, we have four lamentations followed by a prayer of the prophet Jeremiah. Furthermore, the Talmud (see Glossary) as well as many church fathers and theologians, including Luther and Calvin, argue that Jeremiah is the author of the book.

Lamentations is very relevant to the situation in the Middle East. It can be a foundation stone for our theology. My assumption is that the destruction of Jerusalem during the time of Jeremiah is similar to the al-Nakba War (1947–1949) and the series of catastrophes that some Middle Easterners experience today. Based on Lamentations, we will highlight three areas: there is no comforter, there is no prophet and there is no hope.

First, there is no comforter. Lamentations addresses the destruction of the socio-religious infrastructure of ancient Israel.[3] The text describes the besieging of Jerusalem, its famine, its invasion by a powerful army, the execution of its

---

2. See, for example, Adele Berlin, *Lamentations*, The Old Testament Library (Louisville: Westminster John Knox, 2004); Kathleen O'Connor, *Lamentations and the Tears of the World* (New York: Orbis, 2003); or Colin Chapman, "A Lament over Lebanon," Breaking All the Rules Forum, 23 August 2006, accessed 1 December 2017, http://batrneoconwatch.blogspot. co.uk/2006/08/lament-over-lebanon-by-rev-colin.html.

3. For further information, see Robin Parry, *Lamentations* (Kindle ed.; Grand Rapids: Eerdmans, 2010), 112.

leaders, the exile of its people, the looting of its religious places and the collapse of any hope. It simply states that there is no comforter. Lamentations keeps repeating this statement: there is no comforter (Lam 1:2, 9, 16, 17, 21). No one can help the people to deal with their pain and pitiful realities. No one is showing them mercy or compassion, or offering them encouragement and hope in the midst of their troubles. Likewise, there is no comforter for Palestinians, Syrians, Iraqis or members of other nations in similar situations. Israelis are not going to resolve their problems; nor is the Arab world, the Europeans or the Islamic world (see Glossary); the United Nations is not going to help them. The world has abandoned them. There is no comforter. Therefore, we lament.

Second, there is no prophet. The text says that "the law is no more, and her prophets no longer find visions from the LORD" (Lam 2:9). God is silent and people are suffering. This has led to many reactions. Some rightly ask: Where is God? There is no doubt that many people in the Middle East have rejected God because he did not protect them. As a Christian, I prefer to accuse God instead of boycotting him or acting as if he did not exist. Some in Lamentations believed that God had rejected them. Lamentations starts with a question about the suffering of the city, but ends with a question about the endurance of God's rejection (Lam 1:1; 5:19–22). Some preferred the path of self-pity, adopting a victim mentality that wanted all people to see their pain (Lam 1:12). Some preferred the path of revenge (Lam 1:22; 3:64): they dehumanized their enemies in order to facilitate destroying them. However, as Christians, we cannot abandon the logic of love that prompts us to seek justice without abandoning the human dignity of all humanity: revenge is not our path.

Third, Lamentations depicts a reality in which there is no hope. It reminds us of the sign on the gates of hell in Dante's *Divine Comedy*: "Through me you pass into the city of woe . . . All hope abandon ye who enter here."[4] In Palestine, Israel, Syria and many other countries in the Middle East we have an impossible task as we seek to find a political hope. However, the book of Lamentations points out that hope does not depend on the circumstances but on seeing the divine perspective. A prophetic vision is indispensable for the existence of hope. The Palestinian Kairos Document, which was referred to in chapter 1, has a welcome prophetic voice following in the footsteps of those who affirm faith, hope and love (1 Cor 13:13). In 1 Corinthians, these three virtues are found in the literary unit of chapters 12 to 15, which concludes with a strong message of hope rooted in the resurrection of Jesus Christ.

---

4. Dante Alighieri, *The Divine Comedy of Dante Alighieri*, trans. Henry Francis Cary (Whitefish: Kessinger, 2004), 13.

Furthermore, we follow in the footsteps of Saint Augustine. In his *Enchiridion*, or *Handbook*, he points out that hope is born of faith.[5] Hope cannot exist without faith. He adds that "he who does not love believes in vain, even if what he believes is true; he hopes in vain . . . unless he believes and hopes for this: that he may through prayer obtain the gift of love."[6] Love unites us to God.[7] Love does not mean abandoning justice; it means pursuing justice with the logic of love, not revenge. Good hope cannot exist without faith and love. Lamentations says:

> Yet this I call to mind
> and therefore I have hope:

> Because of the LORD's great love we are not consumed,
> for his compassions never fail.
> They are new every morning;
> great is your faithfulness.
> I say to myself, "The LORD is my portion;
> therefore I will wait for him."

> The LORD is good to those whose hope is in him,
> to the one who seeks him;
> it is good to wait quietly
> for the salvation of the LORD.
>
> (Lam 3:21–26)

This hope is confirmed and embodied in the book of Acts. God inflicted pain on Jerusalem, as described in Lamentations, and first-century Jerusalem responded by killing the Messiah of Israel. However, the triune God ended this cycle of violence through faith, love and hope. The Father loved us and offered his only begotten Son on the cross. The Son wept over Jerusalem and suffered at its hands, but he forgave and embodied the path of love. Then the Holy Spirit came to the disciples in Jerusalem. The Holy Spirit is the comforter who will end our exile from God and will grant us a prophetic vision, one not rooted in an ethnocentric reality nor limited to one group, whether Greeks or Hebrews;

---

5. Saint Augustine, *Handbook on Faith, Hope, and Love*, trans. Albert Outler (Grand Rapids: Christian Classics Ethereal Library, n.d.), 76; accessed 12 December 2016, www.ccel.org/ccel/augustine/enchiridion.pdf.

6. Augustine, *Handbook*, 78.

7. See 1 Clement 49:5; Saint Clement, *The First Epistle of Clement to the Corinthians*, trans. J. B. Lightfoot (Athena: Athena Data Products, 1990), 24; accessed 12 December 2016, www.ntslibrary.com/PDF%20Books/First%20Epistle%20of%20Clement%20to%20the%20Corinthians.pdf.

instead, we are witnesses and prophets to the whole world (Acts 1:7–8). Middle Eastern Christians are walking in the footsteps of the early church, advocating faith, love and hope. Hope is accessible to all who call upon the name of the Lord (Acts 2:21). Our witness is indispensable if the church is to continue to embody the power of biblical faith, love and hope to Muslims, Jews and other faith communities. The multi-ethnic church continues to be God's hands to help the poor, challenge oppressive powers, fight discrimination and spread the comfort of God to the ends of the earth. We are a sign of hope.

The following important lessons for Christians flow from this. First, we can cry in the midst of catastrophes. Lamenting is not a sign of hopelessness: it is human and it helps us to maintain our humanity as we mourn with those who are mourning. We need to cry together and to cry as an expression of our commitment to pursue justice and human dignity with the logic of love.

Second, we will not abandon good hope. Those who abandon hope will also abandon the pursuit of justice. A bad hope will lead to suicidal revenge. In contrast, a good hope will remind us of God's mercy and that we are covenant creatures, his people. Christians are a covenant people who can expect the blessings of God despite the forces of death. The structures of injustice will eventually collapse because Babel (Babylon) will fall and the heavenly Jerusalem will come down (Gen 11:5–9; Rev 21:2).

Third, we will commit ourselves to faith, hope and love. Our hope is not wishful thinking or naïve optimism; nor is it founded on the typhonic political atmosphere. Our hope is founded on the nature of our God who conquered death, established the church of the martyrs and promised to be with us. Hope is the bridge that will help us to move from the current reality to the longed-for reality. It is a force of change that rehumanizes people who have been slaves to the forces of dehumanization. It can only be a good change when it is accompanied by faith and love and submission to the Holy Spirit. It is not a surprise that Middle Eastern prophetic voices insist on human dignity from the perspective of faith, asserting that all human beings are created in the image of God, affirming the logic of love and choosing good hope.

Devotional Pause: Psalm 27 (by Gary Nelson)

We pause our tour of the Middle East to look at a psalm.

You lead differently in times of complexity. Even the way change happens is different, often emerging from the most unlikely places, and rarely from the top down. Our experience of God in such times is also different. A very devout and stylish woman shared her story with me [Gary Nelson] which included bouts of severe and sudden depression that clouded every aspect of her life. Nothing seemed to stem the tide nor the inevitability of those regularly occurring times; yet she appeared able to live in the midst of what many would have found debilitating. When asked how she did so, her answer was emphatic: "I decided," she said, "that if this is the life that I am obliged to live, then I will live faithfully and suffer well" – an example of faithfulness and courage in the midst of deeply challenging times. Sometimes all we have in these moments is what we believe about God and the way that he works.

Psalm 27 speaks to this. It focuses on the juxtapositions of faith and fear, security and insecurity. It points to the need for us to nurture sacred memories and signposts that become touchstones in our darkest moments and provide grounding anchors in the midst of the storms.

The psalmist describes his circumstances in the first verse: he is stumbling and falling and afraid that his enemies will overcome him. In the midst of his fear, however, he remembers that what happens to him is not the main thing. That is not his concern. He needs to remember that his life, no matter what the circumstances, rests and is rooted in God. He says, "my heart will not fear . . . I will be confident" (Ps 27:3).

He has one request: for a place, for security. He expresses humanity's deepest desire: to know where to call home. In verse 5 home is described as something other than a geographic location: it is a place to hide in the sense of resting; a place of grace, of God's goodness. The New Testament speaks of our being "hidden with Christ" and our abiding in Christ (e.g. John 15:4; Col 3:3).

The psalmist continues the rhythm of this song moving from praise and adoration in verse 6 to the anxious fears of being abandoned and left homeless (vv. 7–10). In verse 7 the mood changes again from a sense of being held by God to hanging on. The psalmist is being heard despite being alone and feeling rejected and racked by self-doubt.

The pendulum swing from confidence and courage to fears and anxieties represents the real things of life. Living courageously and being able to respond to crisis, chaos and complexity does not mean the absence of these polar-opposite experiences; these are part of the stuff of life.

A friend once said, "The future belongs to those who have nothing to lose." Radical discipleship is found in the lived experience of feelings of home and homelessness. There you discover that hospitality, forgiveness and the living out of the kingdom values outlined in the beatitudes (Matt 5:3–12) are possible. In chapter 1 Aydin illustrated this with his example of radical hospitality, and in chapter 2 Greg Butt defined hospitality as loving an enemy like a brother or sister.

In verses 10 and 11 the psalmist asks God how to live. In verses 13 and 14 his secure confidence in God is clear. Many of us know that God cannot do great things through someone who has not first been greatly broken. Confidence and faith in God are usually forged in the dark places. Kamel, whose story we read in chapter 2, provided an example of this.

Cross-Check: Syria as a Wake-up for the Church (by Nehla Issac)

All of this is illustrated as we resume our tour of the Middle East with a perspective from the Syrian crisis in all of its messiness. Nehla Issac lives in Damascus. As she spoke in the sanctuary of Beirut in June 2017, parts of her city were being bombed. For Damascus, and elsewhere in Syria, armed conflict had become the norm, with numerous parties participating in a seemingly endless cycle of violence. Many such parties had their supporters and suppliers in the region and beyond. For many Syrians, our theme in this chapter of hopelessness and despair was a daily reality: many were asking whether there is a comforter or a prophet or source of hope. Let us hear Nehla's perspective on how the church needs to respond. She begins with a contemporary version of one of Jesus's parables.

Rima, Khadija, Issa and Ali were four children to whom the world's thieves and criminals had paid an invasive visit, stealing their security, joy and peace. They killed their father, took their mother as a war captive, raped the sister and kidnapped the brother. Then they dispensed with the remaining wreckage, these four children, leaving them on the side of the road, with the sidewalk for a mattress, a stone for a pillow and water drops stained a milky colour for food.

A priest passed by muttering words that were meaningless, but they were sufficient to articulate the indifference of the clergy: indeed, he was preoccupied with the delusion that his garments and position defined him. Later, a Levite passed. Bewildered, he expressed his revulsion at what things had come to; yet his hands remained clasped behind his back, out of either helplessness or plain lack of interest. All the while, these children dwelt in the valley of tears, abandoned on the streets of suffering and destitution, hopelessly waiting for the Good Samaritan (Luke 10:25–37). This is what Lamentations embodies as time goes by, as Yohanna discussed above.

Today, one of the biggest challenges for the Arab world, and for Syria specifically, is the shock resulting from the cycle of pain and suffering, which was once far from happening. That is why we earnestly cry out for help, asking, "Is there hope? Should we wait for a comforter? And where is the church's prophetic role?"

In the midst of suffering, the church is an integral part of society: it cannot detach itself and must have a real presence at the heart of the storm. This is why the following question stands out: Can everything we have learned and taught be applied in real life? Or does it lead us only to dilemmas, disputes and difficult questions? The most important questions are: Does God really care? Does he listen? And does he even exist?

It is not uncommon to see true servants of God doing nothing except philosophically defending the existence of God and the fact that he cares and has not forgotten us. At best, it is as if they are watching and waiting, without hope, for a radical change on earth.

Yet the most important challenge that the church faces today is the struggle of its servants and children to stand firm and to live according to moral, divine standards that act as a living testimony to God's perfect righteousness and his unfailing plan for us. The darkness has become closer and darker. In some areas, it has penetrated the church, which, in some places, has turned into just another relief organization: it has become busy collecting and spending funds in its attempt to respond to crises. While this appears to be a good cause, it can divert the children of light from their ultimate goal. This is why we find it difficult to evaluate the effectiveness of relief work, and it has led us to adopt the philosophy of presenting the message of Jesus through social and relief work. Done with the right motivation, this allows the church to fulfil its original and primary role of presenting Christ's message of salvation.

Courage in confronting the enemy requires that we truly understand his strategy. Our enemy, Satan, is cunningly preparing to attack, through whatever means available, the purity, faithfulness and work of the church. That is why we see that the church has missed the target today; it has occupied itself in worldly solutions such as taking part in political ideological debate and similar fields. In doing so it offers a painkiller rather than eradicating the root of all problems, which is the evil widespread in the world. No one can fight this evil except the church.

What was once mainly a positive aspect of Syria – the cultural, racial and political diversity – has turned into a negative one that currently presents a challenge because of the different opinions on the solution for Syria's crisis. Sadly, this richness of diversity has led to conflicts that have worn people down and led to the collapse of the system. Because of pain, suffering and hunger, our Christian community is tired of empty promises and solutions that have mostly failed. This leads us to the vital question: Did God allow this so people might discover the extent of their spiritual, psychological and intellectual hunger? We are a people who seemed to be believing, intellectual and cultured before the crisis; but the winds blew and the masks fell off. This, then, is a chance for the children of God to perform a different kind of work in Syria – a work that proclaims the light of God in the darkness of politics, and the certain solution of Christ as opposed to other delusional solutions.

We might be yoked and subject to corruption and oppression, just like the people of God long ago. We might be weeping and lamenting because of the astonishing hypocrisies we witness, the general sense of indifference and the oppression inflicted by those who were once close to us. That is the cruellest kind of oppression. However, in the light of God's promises, we believe that we are part of God's unfailing project. He is able to reshape us and show us things we overlooked as we were passing through the wilderness of our pain. That is why we persist, why we stay in Syria, certain that tomorrow will be a declaration of victory and not the making of it. It is the acceptance of God's plan and solutions rather than running after other solutions that are like wicker baskets that cannot hold water because of their many holes.

Paul had several enforced pauses for contemplation while in prison. Likewise, I hope that the Syrian crisis will lead us to contemplate that the security we had found in the past had led us to a form of happiness which was no more than an elusive, temporal goal. Furthermore, we now need to spread God's word. This endeavour needs a lot of drive and a lot of compromise. All our current circumstances have led us to despair and tears as we witness the death that our sons and daughters are reaping as they lie in our streets. Then there is the economy that collapsed on our heads, leaving behind financial burdens, familial disputes, divorces and conflicts within the church, as Pastor Harout described in chapter 2. But, for us, these circumstances are an opportunity to mature. Then the church can perform its prophetic, healing role and say with the prophet Isaiah, "The Spirit of the Sovereign LORD is on me, because the LORD has anointed me to proclaim good news to the poor" (Isa 61:1). I can attest, from experience, that the role of the church is very effective in these exceptional circumstances, for it manifests the work, power and certain provision of God.

What the prophet Jeremiah said can also be true of us: "My people have committed two sins: They have forsaken me, the spring of living water, and have dug their own cisterns, broken cisterns that cannot hold water" (Jer 2:13). Today, we boast of civilizations, cultures and accomplishments that cannot hold water. We are called to shake off the dust of worldliness and human solutions, and to seek God's immediate intervention. We are in deep need of a church that not only prays but also shows its unity as it genuinely fights, as one soul and one spirit, towards achieving the heavenly goal. We need to turn our pain into a testimony of our salvation and the manifestation of God's justice in judging the wicked.

Coming back to Rima, Khadija, Issa and Ali, who represent our tragic reality, we see that the Good Samaritan is called to our sidewalks, in order to carry the oil of love and the gospel of peace, and to lift the wounds of our people to the throne of God's providence for a divine work that transcends our reality.

We are in deep need of the basic elements for living. Prior to 2011, Syria boasted that there was not a poor person on its streets. In 2017 it was categorized as one of the neediest countries in the world. Therefore, it is necessary for the church to feed and support the Syrian people. It is also necessary for us to look for new, urgent solutions that suit the Arab world. Previously, we used to suggest solutions that we did not implement; that is why we failed to rid ourselves of the region's core problems that were articulated in the Arab Spring. Solutions that work in the West rarely work here. Our Arab world is going through a fearful challenge: Shari'a (see Glossary) underlies many of our laws. Efforts to solve widespread problems such as the rape of young girls and the exploitation and abuse of the homeless have failed. This is largely because our laws are timeworn, ineffective and shackled. We see the West, on the other hand, overcoming such problems, to a great extent, through its enforced laws. It is most concerning that the church in our country has been inactive for a long time and, even today, still remains largely silent. This is why we must find voices that fight and strive to modernize laws and change what has impeded the advancement of our nation. The timber that kindled the blazing fire in our country includes corruption, bribery and favouritism. For society as a whole, such acts may be normalized, but they have led to the distortion of values within the church: the church is unable to perceive its possible ruin and downfall. This is why we must quickly move together as a church community in order to overcome this epidemic.

Finally, I am certain that what we need most are hearts in which the healing love of God is poured out and his sympathy and compassion dwell. Then we may say that Syria has come back to life and the stone of impossibility has been rolled away. Then we shall see that hope is in the power of waiting faith, the active power of changing love and the acceptance that all humans are made in God's image that was ravished by Satan. Love must be seen in action so that the foe is liberated and turned into a friend. Then the church will have its prophetic voice, a voice that declares that the dignity of any person requires from us a perspective of faith, so we may ascertain that the logic of love is the working power and that hope is the harbour in this storm.

The Book of Psalms for Situations of Conflict and Overt Evil (by Yohanna Katanacho)

The Syrian situation is one of intense suffering for many. It is a situation in which one longs for justice, cries for justice, but has few, if any, channels for confronting the sources causing pain for so many. In chapter 1 and previously in this chapter we described the longstanding and ongoing situation of the Palestinian people. Yohanna Katanacho adds the following reflection on how to live amidst tensions of continuing suffering and persistent cries for justice.

We, Palestinians in Israel–Palestine, live in an ongoing tension: we face a reality of oppression and constantly call for justice. Do not think of this as a negative; be positive: it gives us a chance to love, to go, to disappoint and to be humble. We are sinners and saints simultaneously, both part of the problem and part of the solution. We must bring Christ into the centre of these tensions. The book of Psalms, taken as a whole, is instructive for us.

Psalm 1 is a dream, expressing a desired situation, a reality that does not exist. In contrast, Psalm 73 describes the situation in which we live: one in which the evil are active and the righteous are in pain. We endure a journey of pain, but we are not stuck in the pain since we will live in God's love and will experience his peace one day. We sing in the reality of the cross and the resurrection. But we are not yet in heaven where there is no presence of evil. How can we move towards Psalm 150, which describes the reality of heaven?

Psalm 73 is part of the Asaph group, which comprises Psalms 50 and 73–83. These describe despair, including the desire to kill the non-holy.[8] They also describe God bringing about an end to the unrighteous, and an end to suffering and despair. Psalm 87 shows how a culture of love and justice can break the cycle of violence.[9]

---

8. Yohanna Katanacho, "Peaceful or Violent Eschatology? A Palestinian Christian Reading of the Psalter," in *Christ at the Checkpoint: Theology in the Service of Justice and Peace*, ed. Paul Alexander (Eugene: Wipf & Stock, 2012), 154–172.

9. Yohanna Katanacho, "Jerusalem Is the City of God: A Palestinian Reading of Psalm 87," in *The Land Cries Out*, ed. Salim Munayer and Lisa Loden (Eugene: Wipf & Stock, 2012), 181–199.

We should remove the concept of minority from our thinking, replacing it with a clear recognition of being part of society. We should stop playing the part of victims, as discussed in chapter 1, and become agents and apostles of peace, justice and love. The thought of a Middle East without Christians must prompt us to remind ourselves of God's desires for us and for the region of which we are a part. It is clear that God wants everyone to hear of his love for them. We are part of God's purposes. We must replace any mindset of superiority with one of humility and clear love for all.

Witness 1: Rebecca with Suzanne, Teresa and Fr Simon

We resume our tour of the region with a visit to Egypt. This section describes a number of situations in which individuals and a whole suburb of Cairo have been lifted from hopelessness and despair to having a sense of hope in the present and for the future. Transformation can come. One theme in the stories that follow is that hope came largely from within: people and communities were enabled to use what they had to change their own situation. The role of resources from outside was minimal.

Rebecca was born in Haiti, of Canadian missionary parents. She married Ramez in Canada, then moved to Egypt in 1980 with him and their two small children. We met Ramez in chapter 1 and again briefly in chapter 2.

Rebecca defines despair as having no hope and being unable to do anything to change or improve one's situation. In Egypt she has met numerous people who were in despair. Some have now moved out of despair. One feature of such transformations is the ability to praise God. Isaiah 61:1–3 speaks of the Spirit of the Lord as a garment of praise: praise counteracts despair. Words of praise are heard from people's lips all the time in Egypt; they are part of the cultural norms. Crucial, though, is whether the words are coming from the heart, from a strong sense of belief and trust in God's goodness.

Suzanne is a woman in a very difficult situation; yet she is full of praise to the God she worships. She is Sudanese and moved to Egypt to escape conflict and personal abuse. Rebecca first met her in 2011 at about the time that Suzanne's sister, aged twenty-nine, died leaving six children. Suzanne bravely took the children to her home, in addition to her own two. Her mother moved to Egypt from Sudan to assist. Suzanne's sister's husband also came and was able to provide some financial support, but then he died suddenly. Suzanne suffers from diabetes, a condition not helped by her limited access to medical care. Part of one of her feet had to be amputated, ending her ability to work as a cleaner. She has experienced prejudice and abuse during her years in Egypt, including being punched by a man on a bus simply because of the colour of her skin. (Racial prejudice is common, although few racists express it with physical violence in a public place. Gender-based violence is another form of abuse that needs challenging in Egypt and elsewhere.)

The family applied for refugee status with the UNHCR (see Glossary) with the hope of being resettled in the USA. Her estranged husband heard about this application and suddenly came from Sudan to join his family as a means of securing his entry into another country. This necessitated all the paperwork and application being rewritten. The husband was faithful and supportive for a while before abandoning his wife and family. He did, though, remain within the UNHCR process.

Suzanne's mother also then died, requiring further adjustments to the UNHCR paperwork. As is all too typical, this process took a long time and remained ongoing in summer 2017.

Suzanne is an example of a person maintaining a sense of hope despite the numerous difficulties in her past and present.

Rebecca first went to the Mokattam Garbage Village in Cairo in 1982. Then it was a ghetto rather than a village, where people, animals and garbage shared the same space. All buildings had only one storey. Inhabitants existed by collecting rubbish using donkeys and carts, sorting it, feeding scraps to their animals and selling what they could recycle to make a small income. The only services were tea houses which also sold alcohol and drugs.

The area has been transformed in less than thirty years. This radical transformation came from the people themselves; it did not come from government action or foreign aid or charities. How did this occur?

It began in 1974. Although all residents of the Garbage Village were Christians in name, there was no church building there, nor Bibles or schools. A man now called Father Simon went there and started preaching. He consistently spoke about Jesus, emphasizing that Jesus valued them highly, enough to have died for them. This was in sharp contrast to the message being given by the wider society whose rubbish they collected and who treated them so badly that the garbage collectors thought of themselves as no better than garbage.

Fr Simon's teaching and the resultant conversions of the residents gave them a greater sense of self-worth and led to changed behaviour. For example, sales of alcohol and drugs were drastically reduced. The income being earned was now available for other uses. Better homes were constructed and a school and medical services were initiated. These new activities also created employment opportunities for the women of the area. The first church was constructed in the late 1970s and was the first building to have more than one storey. Many years later the church at the Garbage Village discovered many caves in the cliffs in their area and turned them into places of worship. These are now referred to as the "Cave Churches of the Garbage Village," and you can even find them on Google. The largest one can hold 20,000 people, making it the largest church "building" in the Middle East. The Cave Churches attract many visitors into the area each day.

By the early 2000s most of the donkeys and carts had been replaced with trucks. The scale of the recycling activities has grown, although most of the sorting is still done by hand. Most buildings are now multi-storey and traffic jams have become a challenge.

One individual in this context is Teresa. Her husband died young, leaving her with two small children. Shortly afterwards, her father also died and Teresa was left with no male relative able to provide for the family. She responded by working during the day as a cleaner and going to night school in the evening. She flourished, becoming first a teacher and then the first person to introduce a Montessori curriculum within the church school.[10] Rooted in her story is praise rather than despair.

Rebecca has learned much from Suzanne and Teresa, two people who have lived for others not just themselves: two people who believe that God is in control despite the evidence to the contrary in their situations.

We met Ramez, Rebecca's husband, in chapter 1. A few years ago Ramez's secretary told him that Adel the "garbage collector" had come to meet him. Ramez wondered why someone would describe himself as a garbage collector. Adel came dressed in a smart business suit. Having been transformed by the power of the gospel, he knew that his task of collecting, sorting and recycling garbage was his job and it did not define him as a person. So he was no longer embarrassed to say what he did since it did not reflect on who he now knew himself to be. He now dressed and behaved like a professional person.

Most people resident in the Garbage Village in 2017 were happy to be there: they appreciated a sense of community that is rare elsewhere. In recent years, some Muslims had chosen to move to the area, which had become a small city.

---

10. The Montessori method of education was developed by Dr Maria Montessori and seeks to develop the social, emotional and physical abilities of children as well as their cognitive abilities. It is rooted in the innate aptitude of everyone to seek knowledge and to develop ways of learning given a supportive and conducive environment.

Many residents felt a sense of empowerment, a sense of control of their lives. Children were safe (except from traffic!) and the vast majority were aware that they were known and loved. Many adults were involved in being supportive of one another. There were exceptions to this positive picture and further work continued to be initiated. One example was support for the chronically ill and disabled, much of which was initiated by the youth of the church. An eight-storey centre for such work was completed in the 2010s. This is an example of how responding to disorienting times requires a different style of leadership. This is where Rebecca now devotes most of her time.

Witness 2: Nadia with Tala and Sahar

We switch country once more, moving to Lebanon. This diverse country has many who are prosperous as well as others who are impoverished.

Nadia Khouri Accad is part of an organization providing health, education and social services within an economically disadvantaged suburb of Beirut. She notes that Katanacho's contribution on the book of Lamentations provides us with a deeply compassionate perspective followed by a powerful call to action in the most practical and human sense.

Katanacho divides this call to action into three parts. First, he reaffirms the need to mourn in the midst of catastrophe, claiming that this mourning, these salty tears, are essential to preserving our very humanity. A verse in the introductory poem says that "Pouring tears of mercy and compassion is true piety." Second, he goes on to remind us to have hope in the midst of pain – but a good hope, a divinely inspired hope, that is stubborn in the pursuit of justice. And third, it is the practical expression of this good hope that acts as a pathway and reminder of God's mercy. It is this hope that helps us to move from the current reality to the hoped-for reality. He writes that this hope "is a force of change that rehumanizes people who have been slaves to the forces of dehumanization."

According to Nadia Khouri Accad, Dr Katanacho's paper articulates well the force of God-given hope which drives much compassion work, including that of the organization she is involved with. It works with families facing extreme economic and social conditions in Beirut. It is located in an area that is "off the grid," so to speak, where there is no policing and no public services. It is perceived as an unsafe neighbourhood, a "no-go zone," not only by many other organizations and service providers, but even by the authorities who enter the neighbourhood only to make arrests. The organization has been operating in the neighbourhood for over fifteen years, offering educational, health and social services. It has become a core part of the neighbourhood's fabric. The fuel for this work was a stubborn "good hope" that families might move out of crippling poverty to a new reality where they would be able to realize their full human potential, unconstrained by economic and social oppression.

The first-hand accounts of two individuals involved in this work reflect what Dr Katanacho's call to action implies, both at the personal and community levels. Specifically, these illustrate the lived experiences of those going through adversity or of those who accompany them daily as they experience hardship. These experiences highlight the personal development that often grows out of adversity as well as stubborn, persistent good hope in God's mercy.

Tala is Syrian. Her childhood was difficult, not least after her father left the home when she was twelve. At that point, Tala left school to work and provide for her mother and siblings. Tala longed to study and so saved some of her wages, bought books and started studying at home after work. She also used some of her wages to pay for a private tutor to help her. One day she returned from work to discover her books had been burnt by her sister and her mother, emphasizing the requirement to work, not study. Tala found the courage to replace the books and hide them at her place of work, a clinic. Tala would study during her lunch breaks in secret. One day her boss, a physician, found out. Instead of reprimanding her, she encouraged and supported her. Tala persisted in studying in secret and was able to complete her high-school degree.

The eruption of the Syrian crisis affected Tala, as it has so many families. By 2011 she was married and had her own children. The family was forced to move often within Syria to escape the violence and economic hardship. However, a breaking point came for them when Tala's husband was captured. At great risk to her own safety, Tala tried to negotiate his release – sadly, to no avail. Others tried to help but also failed. The situation became increasingly dangerous. She recalls feeling total despair and calling out to God for help as she walked the city streets looking for a way forward. She felt led to a nearby shop where she happened to meet a good friend of her husband. She told him about the situation. He listened quietly without much reaction. Tala returned home to her children. Five hours later, this friend returned with her husband, having crossed dangerous enemy lines and risked his own life to save him. Tala regards both these experiences as answers to prayer, to her cry of despair.

Tala's family, like so many others, decided to leave Syria and move to Lebanon. After a few difficult years in Lebanon, her husband made the dangerous journey overland to Germany, but as of summer 2017 had been unable to secure visas for Tala and the children. Tala longs that they can be reunited as a family.

She regards herself as a stronger person because of what she has been through. She is committed most of all to providing an education for her children and to giving them a joyful upbringing.

Sahar is a nurse and a colleague of Nadia's at the same organization's clinic. One day a new patient named Rima, a Syrian refugee, was brought to the clinic. Rima was an eleven-year-old girl born with spina bifida which, among other things, caused her foot to be at a forty-five-degree angle to her body. As a result of walking on her heel, she developed a deep and persistent wound. Sahar treated Rima's wound daily for one year. In a reflective piece about their relationship, she talks about the growth she experienced through those daily encounters with Rima. Most importantly, it caused her to reflect on who was really strong in that relationship: Sahar, who worked in the frequently challenging conditions of the neighbourhood, or Rima. Sahar writes:

> My main "task" was to do a daily dressing on her "bad" foot. Every day for a year, I did my job with her, but I did not realize until recently what she has done to me. She taught me what it is like to be strong:
>> Strong is to have the will to go on living with one leg and crutches and accept the bitter fact.
>> Strong is to have the power to walk from home to the clinic and then to school faster than the remarks and the looks from the little brats.
>> Strong is to keep a smile on your face no matter how tough it gets.
>> Strong is she.

Global Cross-Check: From Hopelessness and Despair to Anger and Courage (by Shane McNary)

Having visited several countries in the region, we now explore the theme of hopelessness and despair in a broader, worldwide context. For this theme we will focus on one ethnic group in central Europe as well as making brief references to situations in sub-Saharan Africa and North America. The following section was provided by Shane McNary, a citizen of the USA living and working in Europe. He introduces us to a people whose language has a very limited vocabulary for hope. He picks up on the theme of chapter 1 of challenging injustice, whether at the level of individuals or structurally within society as a whole due to the attitudes, behaviours and policies of ruling elites. These elites he refers to using the term "Empire" which, in this context, implies the suppression of any who challenge the actions or authority of the rulers.

I think that as long as we are able to remember the promises of God, there is no situation we face where we can say that we are without hope. Hopelessness is a denial of the power of God to keep God's promises to us. Hopelessness is absurd and the impetus for actions resulting in increased suffering and broken relationships. A person who feels hopeless loses meaning and appreciation for life; he or she cannot envision a future different from the present.

In writing about the Arab Spring, Marwan Bishara, al Jazeera English's senior political analyst, described the great shifts in expectations among those who expected swift resolution of the dramatic changes in the Arab world. When the long-term horizon is overwhelmed with short-term views, said Bishara, "myopia masquerading as realism" controls the narrative.[11] When Christians give up hope for the future and live only for today, our myopia offers a distorted view, a false realism and descent into hopelessness. Christian hope pulls us towards tomorrow and does not allow us to be blinded by this myopia.

But what of despair? Jürgen Moltmann reminds us that despair "presupposes hope" and "seek[s] to preserve the soul from disappointments."[12] In difficulties, despair is a reminder that things should not be this way. Despair is not a lack of hope; it is the soul's attempt to express dissatisfaction at the pace of the fulfilment of hope. Despair is our unsuccessful attempt to pull against hope and bring it towards today.

One of our ministries in Slovakia and the Czech Republic is to host short-term ministry teams. With each team we try to introduce them into the wider context where they are working. During 2017 we visited the Auschwitz-Birkenau Holocaust Museum three times. We remembered the horrors of what began as a prison for Polish political prisoners, then became a place for the internment of Roma (see Glossary) families and, finally, was made into an efficient death-machine targeting the Jews from around Europe. On one tour, the guide reminded us of the immense power of hope. However, his words

---

11. Marwan Bishara, *The Invisible Arab: The Promise and Peril of the Arab Revolutions* (New York: Nation Books, 2013), 238.

12. Jürgen Moltmann, *Theology of Hope* (New York: Harper & Row, 1967), 23.

were a warning about the manipulation of hope. He stated, "The perpetrators used hope as a weapon against the people." Sometimes the work of Empire is to turn hope into a weapon to be used against the people. Promises of peace, of freedom, of safety and of making Empire great again are employed, manipulating hope into a useful force for the purposes of Empire.

The communist era in Slovakia (1945–1989) turned spouses into informants and pastors into spies through the work of the secret police, by offering a false utopian realism that stole hope from two generations of people who forgot how to dream of a different or better way of life. Today (mid-2017), neo-Nazis have returned to parliament in Slovakia. Though they are not part of the ruling coalition, their influence continues to grow as they offer a cynical, twisted hope of a racially pure country free from refugees, from NATO and from the Roma. Allan Aubrey Boesak comments, "When politicians speak of hope, it is political pietism for the sake of expediency. . . . When politicians speak of hope, it is with the certitude of power."[13]

I was in Osijek, Croatia, walking with a friend along the beautiful Drava River when I noticed the marks on the pavement. "Where did these come from?" I asked. "That is from when the Serbians were bombing our city." Little more than a generation ago the evil of ethnic and religious purity once again ripped apart the fabric of society in parts of Europe. And let us not forget the horrific experience of the Tutsi women and children who sought shelter in a church only to have the preacher encourage the soldiers outside: "I bless this killing! I bless you for ridding this country of another cockroach!"[14] How is it possible not to lose hope? How do we deal with the experience of despair in these times?

Our ministry is with the Roma people. Misunderstood and despised, they have been in Central Europe for six hundred years and still live as outcasts. It is said about the Roma that they live only for today. With them, it is "feast or famine." If you have money, you spend it all quickly and enjoy the feast. I am on the board of a Slovak organization that has translated the New Testament into a Roma dialect spoken in Slovakia. Because the dialect is not a rich language, some words which have been replaced over time by Slovak words are not known to most speakers. When "hope" was translated – for example, in 1 Corinthians 13:13 – the unfamiliar Roma word was used and in parentheses

---

13. Allan Aubrey Boesak, *Dare We Speak of Hope? Searching for a Language of Life in Faith and Politics* (Grand Rapids: Eerdmans, 2014), 138.

14. Boesak, *Dare We Speak of Hope?*, 124; citing Immaculée Ilibagiza, *Left to Tell: Discovering God amidst the Rwandan Holocaust* (Carlsbad, CA: Hay House, 2006 & 2014).

the Slovak word for "hope" was added for clarity. This led some to believe that in the Roma language there is no word for hope. This is not true. What is true is that many have learned to live in a constant state of despair and hopelessness because they have grown so accustomed to disappointment and distrust in the justice of nature, governments and laws.

The experience of African Americans is also a story of despair and hopelessness. Even in 2017, 150 years after the abolition of slavery and fifty years after the Civil Rights Movement (see Glossary) brought an end to the official discrimination of the Jim Crow era, the experience of many black-skinned people in America is still filled with despair. Wendell Griffen provides a sobering illustration: "In the United States, the prison-industrial-capitalist complex has grown into an $86 billion business. A young person of color walking down the street is absolutely worthless to the wealthy and the powerful. . . . Once in prison though, he or she becomes a capital-generating commodity of great worth. An inmate will generate between $30,000 to $40,000 per year in profits for the privatized prison system. Only when they can be turned into profits do they count."[15]

The experience of non-white people in apartheid South Africa also testifies to the determination of hope against the continued onslaught of oppression, racism and crimes against humanity. It is from that setting that Allan Aubrey Boesak reminds us that "Hope is found where Jesus is to be found, this Jesus who was despised and rejected, whose countenance, like the faces of the wretched of the earth, no one desires to gaze upon."[16] The presence of hope in the face of despair has been illustrated in a fantastic way in a painting entitled *Hope* by George Frederic Watts.[17]

Jesus was there when ethnic or sectarian violence mutated neighbours into enemies in Rwanda and the former Yugoslavia. He was there even in the midst of despair and the absurdity of hopelessness. Indeed, it is at these precise times that Jesus – Emmanuel, God with us – "participates in the human struggle for liberation from oppression in all its forms."[18] Where freedom of religion or belief for all is denied, resulting in despair, Jesus is there demanding justice. It is the purpose of God and the mission of the church to seek liberation and justice. "The Jesus that we find in the biblical Gospels incites us both

---

15. Wendell L. Griffen, *The Fierce Urgency of Prophetic Hope* (Valley Forge: Judson, 2017).

16. Boesak, *Dare We Speak of Hope?*, 80.

17. See, for example, https://en.wikipedia.org/wiki/Hope_%28painting%29, accessed 7 November 2017.

18. Griffen, *Fierce Urgency*, 42.

to proclaim the gospel of repentance and forgiveness and to hope, pray and struggle for liberation and justice."[19]

Our faith compels us to seek the transformation of oppression into liberation, of slavery into freedom, of hopelessness into hope. We do this through the proclamation of the good news and seeking justice. The response of Christians is not to turn away in despair from the injustice of atrocities, but to strive for justice and reconciliation for all.

In the words of Saint Augustine of Hippo, "Hope has two beautiful daughters. Their names are Anger and Courage. Anger at the way things are, and courage to see that they do not remain the same."[20] As Christians of conviction and faith, we do not sacrifice either of Hope's daughters. We know Anger when persons who bear the image of God are made inferior through the evil abuses of Empire; and we are not afraid to speak truth to power and demand justice for all with the same courageous dedication of Jesus.

As Raimundo Barreto wrote for the Baptist World Alliance: "In times of great civil strife and violence, Baptists share stories of hope, solidarity, and unselfish commitment to the wellbeing of others inspired by the public witness of many Baptists around the world. These storied lives help equip us to work in solidarity with other victims of injustice and violence in order to promote tolerance, mutual respect, freedom of religion and belief, just relationships, and peaceful coexistence."[21]

We need to embrace both anger and courage. We should not accept injustice, lack of freedom of religion or belief, intolerance and war. These things should cause us to feel anger. But we do not want to embrace only this one daughter of hope. We want also to embrace courage. It takes courage to seek justice for all, and not just for ourselves and for our own. Courage compels us to demand peace, justice and freedom of religion and belief for all. The courage to love our neighbour as ourselves is the same courage we draw from when we speak with prophetic confidence against Empire and injustice.

---

19. Raimundo C. Barreto Jr., Ken Sehested and Luis Rivera-Pagán, eds., *Engaging the Jubilee: Freedom and Justice Papers of the Baptist World Alliance (2010–2015)* (Falls Church, VA: Baptist World Alliance, 2015), 319.

20. Cited by Boesak, *Dare We Speak of Hope?*, 42.

21. Barreto, Sehested and Rivera-Pagán, *Engaging the Jubilee*, xvi.

Responding to Hopelessness and Despair: Four Causes for Hope (by Helen Paynter)

Here we draw together the thoughts expressed in this chapter, together with relevant issues from those that have preceded it. Helen Paynter provided the following reflection based on what we have covered. She is British and lectures at Bristol Baptist College, UK.

It is difficult for me, as someone born into, and living in, a situation of privilege, to speak on the subject of "Hopelessness and Despair." But I have been asked to do so, and on the basis that I am reflecting on what I have observed and noticed, and on Scripture, I will dare to do so.

At least two definitions of despair have been offered to us. Let me work with the one given to us by Rebecca: Despair is found where there is no hope and no credible possibility of hope. Psychologically, despair might be born out of rage or resignation, but in the end it will, I think, be manifest as a flattening of emotions, as a lack of rage, as a lack of hope, as a normalization of suffering.

I have observed many of the companions of despair: guilt, shame, bereavement, loss of possessions, loss of identity, homesickness, fear, pain, humiliation, discord and purposelessness. As one who comes from a background of privilege, I hesitate even to list such sorrows, lest my naming of them should seem to trivialize them. But I do name them, and I honour those for whom they are a daily reality. What do we do with such a list? How can beauty be found in such ashes?

In his excellent book *The Prophetic Imagination*, Walter Brueggemann[22] points out that when Moses perceived the suffering of his people under Pharaoh, the first stage in the liberation process was for him to describe and lament the injustice. Their suffering had become normalized. For us to look on injustice and be indifferent to it is a failure of compassion and a loss of humanity. Further, to look on injustice and fail to be angered by it is a failure of faith. Faith looks on what is, compares it with what should be and believes that there is a God to whom that complaint should be addressed. Faith says, "This is not how God purposed the world to be"; faith cries, "This is not how the world will one day be." The tears and shouts of faith are a protest against the violence, sorrow, injustice and lost-ness of our world.

We should note the diversity of experiences testified to in the consultation. Most of the situations described are the results of complex historical stories.

---

22. Walter Brueggemann, *The Prophetic Imagination* (Minneapolis: Fortress, 2001).

Some are institutional injustice or persecution. In others, the wrongs are perpetrated at grass-roots level. In some, Christians are specifically targeted. In others, Christians are being caught up in a more generalized situation. The same remedy will not work in all cases. Yet in each one, the church of God is being placed under strain and is in pain. Like the psalmist, we lament and cry out, "How long, O Lord?"; and with Habakkuk, "Why do you remain silent?" (e.g. Ps 35:17; Hab 1:2).

Brueggemann encourages us that the next step in the transformative process of liberation is to imagine another reality: to dream that God might break in; to conceive of a world where justice rolls down like a river, and where righteousness and peace kiss each other (Ps 85:10; Amos 5:24).

We dare to believe that such a world is not beyond God's capacity. We even dare to believe that the seeds of that harvest have already been sown, and that the tender green shoots of hope are visible.

So let me name the causes for hope that I have detected in the stories before us. First, I note the glorious capacity of human resilience; that God has endowed us with such creativity, courage and adaptability. So villages rise out of garbage. So those who have fled with only the clothes on their backs find new ways of expressing their dignity. So communities in disarray organize themselves. So education is offered and received. So new, creative ways of non-violent resistance are constantly emerging.

Second, I note the compassion and care of the global church. I note that, despite our tendency to become consumed by our own preoccupations, churches across the world will pray, will give money and will send people to strengthen parts of the body of Christ whom they have never met, yet acknowledge as family.

Third, I note, as I am directed to by my brothers and sisters, that even in the darkest setting, the light of God is not extinguished. I note that the church under persecution is often growing, not fading away. I note that many who have fled their homes, clinging to the tattered shreds of human hope, have discovered to their surprise a solid, eternal hope. I note that the obedience of faithful men and women is a light on a stand in a dark place. I note the courage of those who choose to remain. I note the strength of those who have faithfully suffered torture. I note the forgiveness offered by the violated. I note that the Holy Spirit is still present and active throughout his church, in fulfilment of the last words Jesus spoke before his ascension (Acts 1:8).

Fourth, I note that those who oppress, persecute or abuse the weak or the godly have placed themselves on the wrong side of history. I look back and note the fall of the Roman Empire, the defeat of the Third Reich and the collapse of the Soviet Union. I note that God leans out of heaven to pay attention to the treatment of the weak and the oppressed. I note that the judgment of God will be total, just and merciful, and is very, very sure. I note the new creation that we are already witnessing to, and in which we will one day dance with our Saviour.

But in the meantime, in this time between the times, when we cry Maranatha – "Lord, come quickly" (e.g. Rev 22:20) – the hope that these stories show has strengthened my hope. I will take away the stories and strengthen my church with them, and we will remind ourselves of the glorious, unconquerable reality of the church, in which our Lord reigns by his Spirit.

Leading Prophetically

This chapter has given several examples of the church being the agent of transformation in society. One factor, not always stated or appreciated, is that it frequently requires persistent, consistent, reliable and faithful commitment to those experiencing hopelessness and despair. We remarked in chapters 1 and 2 about the need for determination in pursuing and fulfilling the call of God; this is the case when working on behalf of those facing hopelessness and despair.

In this chapter we have repeated the call of chapter 1 that injustice needs to be confronted by the church. We have also been taken into a situation where challenging rulers acting unjustly is not a viable option for the national church. An analysis of the reasons why this is the case for the Syrian crisis in 2017 will be given in the next chapter. We live with the tension of following a God of justice and at times being obliged to lament and accept that confronting Empire must wait. Further, we must remain vigilant because the opportunity to do so will become viable one day. Until then, what is possible, and is being undertaken by some, is to act to meet the humanitarian needs of the desperate and to make the gospel of Jesus available to anyone who wishes to consider it. It is being present in the midst of hopelessness and despair, sharing the pain and doing what one can to alleviate suffering.

One message is that numerical size is not crucial; being a small part of society does not prevent the church being transformational. We are aware that a little yeast, salt or light transforms its surroundings. What matters is faithfulness. This observation leads us neatly into our final subject. Being a minority is simply a statement of numbers. Being minoritized, that is, being overtly oppressed, is not inevitable: it is a process that can be resisted and challenged prophetically.

Questions for Reflection

1. If to hope means to prophetically seek an alternative reality to the present one, what alternative reality might God be inviting you to imagine for your own situation?

2. How can we lament while being people of faith, hope and love?

3. How can we embrace anger, courage and love in the face of hate, injustice, hopelessness and despair?

4

Minoritization

Our subject in this chapter is minoritization. This is more than marginalization in which people are ignored or overlooked but allowed to get on with their lives in their own communities. The minoritized are being overtly, consciously, unjustly suppressed.

The first contributor in this chapter is Martin Accad. Martin is Lebanese and also holds Swiss nationality. He lives in Lebanon and much of his portfolio of work is based at ABTS (see Contributors). We met his wife Nadia in chapter 3. He draws the distinction between being a minority, simply small in number which is a fact with a history, and being suppressed, which he argues is not inevitable and can and should be resisted.

This will be followed by a contribution from Ehab el-Kharrat, whom we met in the Introduction. He argues that our identity in Christ should underpin our efforts at resisting being minoritized by playing an active and constructive part in society as a whole. Our two witness statements take us to Iraq and then the Palestinian diaspora community in Lebanon. Our global cross-check takes us to France together with a brief look at Canada. Both illustrate Martin Accad's point that no community anywhere is immune to being minoritized.

From Minority Status to the Fateful Embrace of Minoritization (by Martin Accad)

I want to explore "minoritization" as a socio-political and psychological process, in contrast to the more descriptive status simply of being a "minority." For a community to be small in number, or for an individual to belong to a small community, is simply an accident of history, even though it is also related to the way that a group defines itself. But the process of "minoritization" is not a fact of history. It is an intentional process, imposed on an individual or a community either from the inside or from the outside. In this chapter, we are arguing that by challenging prophetically the minoritization process, whether it originated from the inside or from the outside, the "dominant consciousness" of the status quo can be challenged. An alternative divine vision – a "prophetic consciousness" – can be projected, which will lead individuals and their communities towards new horizons and a new perception of their transformative role in society.

The incidence of hopelessness in the general Arab population, particularly among the youth, is very high. Whether it manifests itself through emigration or through young people joining radical violent groups such as ISIS/Daesh or al-Qaeda (see Glossary), these are symptoms of these young people's deeper conviction that there is no future for them or their children, either in their particular country or setting, or in the world. In that sense, the feelings of radical jihadists are, in essence, not so different from the feelings of religious minorities living in the Muslim world. The feeling emerges from the questions of theodicy (see Glossary): "Why does God allow so much evil in the world?" "What about his promises of restoration of all things?" "What hope do we have in a world that offers us and our children so little opportunity?"

Islamist jihadist ideology (see Glossary) provides answers in violence, in a call to take things into one's own hands, often clothing it in pietistic illusions of bringing about God's kingdom in the world before God's own timing. Is it not this way of thinking, that we can accelerate the "coming of God" forcefully, that also feeds the ideology of Zionism? Christians in the MENA region, for the most part, have refused to give in to violence as an answer to theodicy. But instead, some have given in to other forces, such as a life of hopelessness and inability to receive God's calling in their lives. Others have given in to the solution of fleeing from danger and are emigrating, as was discussed in chapter 2. Still others valiantly embrace their fate of persecution, seeding church history with more of their blood, in unity with a long legacy of martyrdom, as discussed in chapter 1.

Numerically speaking, Christians in the Muslim world are of course in the minority today. However, contrary to what is popularly supposed, Christians in Muslim lands historically did not immediately become minorities. Richard W. Bulliet, in a book of just over 150 pages, argued that for several centuries after the rise and expansion of Islam, many of the populations outside Arabia for the most part retained the faith of their ancestors.[1] Although, for a variety of reasons, Christians in North Africa embraced Islam as a single ethnic group

---

1. Richard W. Bulliet, *Conversion to Islam in the Medieval Period: An Essay in Quantitative History* (Cambridge: Harvard University Press, 1979).

towards the end of the first century of Islam (c. 750) and there were mass conversions in Central Asia around the same period, the Muslim populations of Egypt, Iraq and Iran reached about 50 percent only around the year 900. In the regions of Syria and modern-day Turkey, on the other hand, this did not happen until after 1200. Most Albanians and Bosnians, together with some Bulgarians, became Muslims in the fourteenth century under Ottoman expansion, and beginning in 1192, Muslim Turkish tribesmen conquered new parts of India. The Buddhist population of present-day Bangladesh almost entirely and rapidly embraced Islam beginning in the 1300s. Others in Punjab and Kashmir also converted. Traders and Sufis (see Glossary) began to spread Islam in south India, Sri Lanka and south-east Asia from around 1300. Between 1300 and 1500 Islam spread among the Buddhist, Hindu and traditional religions of present-day Indonesia and Malaysia. During that period most of the Turkic-speaking peoples of Central Asia and Mongolia became Muslims, and Islam also entered the western parts of China. On the African continent, between about 990 and 1500 most of the peoples of the African Sahel belt[2] became Muslims. The first town along the Niger River to become Muslim was Gao in modern-day Mali (c. 990). In those regions, conversion happened mainly through traders, travelling Sufis, beginning with the conversion of a ruler, which was soon followed by that of his people. By 1040, several groups in Senegal had become Muslims and took Islam to Senegal, western Mali and Guinea. The Soninke people, founders of the Empire of Ghana (c. 750–1240), converted to Islam through the influence of traders from North Africa around 1076. Islam then spread further east along the Niger River. Islam began to be established around Lake Chad from as early as 1100. In East Africa, by the tenth century, traders had spread Islam along the coast. The population of Nubia, in Sudan, gradually became Muslim during the fourteenth century, and Islam began to spread south of Khartoum only after 1500.

This material challenges the notion that Islam as a religion spread rapidly by the sword as soon as Muslim armies initiated their conquests outside Arabia after the death of Muhammad in 632. In every region, the situation was different. Christians, Hindus, Buddhists and adherents of various traditional religions always began as numerical majorities. And in the face of increasing Muslim conquest and proselytization, they all faced very different forms of pressure – from war to migration, trade, education and preaching – until they eventually shifted to the status of minorities under Muslim rule. In some of

---

2. The Sahel is a semi-arid area stretching from Senegal in the west to Sudan in the east and from the Sahara desert to the north to a belt of savannahs to the south.

these contexts, they quickly came under Muslim rule, whereas in others, the growing Muslim population remained a minority under non-Muslim rule for many centuries. As far as Christian populations were concerned, they lost adherents, sometimes through persecution and forced migration, but more often through gradual conversions.[3] This is not to undermine the significant stress that Christian populations have come under historically as a result of war, forced migration, and social and economic pressures. The recent histories of Turkey, Iraq and Syria have shown us how only a very few years of violent jihad can nearly extinguish a previously vibrant Christian population. In Mosul, Iraq, a city whose vibrant Syriac Christian community persisted for two thousand years, the church bells stopped ringing following Daesh's takeover of the city in August 2014. They were timidly heard again in the vicinity of Qaraqosh after Daesh's ousting by Iraqi coalition forces in autumn 2016.[4] However, what this tells us is that in most cases it is the attitude of church leaders and Christian populations in the face of such pressures that plays a defining role in their own fate.

Even as Christians in the West feel the growing presence of Muslims in their countries, they should give heed to the historical experience of Christian populations in the MENA region. At the moment, Muslims in the West are using primarily legal and media strategies to claim more rights in social contexts where they are still a minority and often feel pressured and minoritized – even sometimes persecuted – by the non-Muslim majority. A very small minority, however, have been using increasingly violent means to intimidate local populations, mainly in the form of terrorist attacks, but also through more aggressive assertiveness in cities where they are becoming majorities. Some observers have argued that Islam remains moderate only until Muslims become the majority. Such perceptions are often accompanied by doom-like warnings that Muslims will not stop using violence until the entire world is subdued to Islam.[5] Historically speaking, such expectations are not entirely unrealistic or far-fetched. However, further analysis should be carried out when comparing different times in history. Which features are

---

3. See, for example, Bulliet, *Conversion to Islam*; and Fred McGraw Donner, ed., *The Expansion of the Early Islamic State* (Aldershot: Ashgate, 2008).

4. See, for example, Bethan McKernan, "Christians Near Mosul Celebrate Their First Mass since Being Liberated from Isis," *The Independent*, 31 October 2016, accessed 5 June 2017, www.independent.co.uk/news/world/middle-east/mosul-offensive-latestchristians-celebrate-mass-after-liberation-from-isis-a7388816.html.

5. E.g. Mark Durie, *The Third Choice: Islam, Dhimmitude and Freedom* (Melbourne: Deror Books, 2010).

common and which are different? What are the main factors contributing to Islam's behaviour one way or another? What factors of history today may drive our disorienting times in a different direction from that of the past? And, perhaps more importantly, what have been the attitudes of MENA Christians historically, and what can we learn from them? What does the Bible teach us, and how should we respond today?

In order to explore these important questions, I will focus on one primary factor, namely, the issue of being a minority in the context of a majority, which I have simply described above as an accident of history. Furthermore, in line with my topic, how does the process of minoritization address the reality of being a minority, and how then should we respond to this reality?

Minoritization as a Process of Subjugation

As we have said, we need to distinguish between minority as a state of being and minoritization as a subjugation process. Insight comes to us from socio-linguistics, particularly from French scholars Deleuze and Guattari, who argue that minorities are "objectively definable states, states of language, ethnicity, or sex with their own ghetto territorialities." However, they argue, minorities "must also be thought of as seeds, crystals of becoming whose value is to trigger uncontrollable movements and deterritorializations of the mean or majority."[6]

Deleuze and Guattari deconstruct our common thinking about the majority/minority dynamic. They universalize the concept of minority as the starting point of any language, gender, ethnic or social group. By their very existence, minority "states of being" are disruptive to dominant majority powers (*pouvoirs*). But they reject the idea that revolution is achieved by "regionalizing" or "ghettoizing" minority consciousness, such as when a minority group adopts a narrow regional dialect as an act of protest. Rather, they argue, it is "by using a number of minority elements, by connecting, conjugating them," that one achieves "a specific, unforeseen, autonomous becoming."[7]

The concept of "majority" implies a "state of domination," regardless of whether this majority is numerically larger than other species, genders or even political groups. It is thus irrelevant that mosquitoes are more numerous in the universe than human beings, or whether women or children are more numerous than men. "The majority in a government presupposes the right

---

6. Gilles Deleuze and Felix Guattari, *A Thousand Plateaus: Capitalism and Schizophrenia* (Minneapolis: University of Minnesota Press, 2005), 106.

7. Deleuze and Guattari, *A Thousand Plateaus*, 106.

to vote, and not only is established among those who possess that right but is exercised over those who do not, however great their numbers." In other words, and as we have been arguing, "It is important not to confuse 'minoritarian,' as a becoming or process, with a 'minority,' as an aggregate or a state."[8]

Based on the Deleuze/Guattari hypothesis, Syrian theologian Najib George Awad, in an article he published in 2014 in the Lebanese Arabic daily newspaper *al-Mustaqbal*, laments and critiques the growing process of marginalization to which Christians of Syria have been subjected since the start of the Syrian War in 2011. In his article, entitled "On the 'Protection of Minorities' and Christians in the Syrian Question," Awad rejects the definition of "minority" as a static ontological descriptor. He argues that "minority" is effectively a status which a group of people attain as a result of a process of "minoritization" (Arabic *aqlala*) imposed on them. Moreover, he argues that this process is applied to the group either actively or passively. The minoritization process is passive when it is self-imposed, when a group chooses to define itself, often on ethical grounds, in opposition and contrast to a social majority perceived as immoral. An active process of minoritization, on the other hand, takes place when a leading political force views anyone opposing its policies as a traitor and unworthy of being part of the society.[9]

Awad uses this lens to argue that, in the Syrian context, all those who have opposed the Assad regime over the past fifty years have been subjected to a process of minoritization, regardless of their sectarian affiliation. Christians, as a numeric minority, have been marginalized due to an unhealthy patron–client relationship that has developed with the state: they have fallen hostage to the state in exchange for "protection" in the face of a presumed danger. Sunnis, though numerically the vast majority, have been effectively the most politically "minoritized" social category under Hafez Assad and Bashar Assad, presidents of Syria from 1970 to 2000 and from 2000 to the present day respectively. Even Alawites (see Glossary), when they have not aligned with the state regime, have been "minoritized" and oppressed, even though they belong to the same sect as the Assad family. In the same way, an oppressive political regime will apply the process of "majoritization" on any individual or group, of any religious or ethnic affiliation, who will support its policies. Such groups and individuals

---

8. Deleuze and Guattari, 291.

9. Nagib George Awad, "On the 'Protection of Minorities' and Christians in the Syrian Question" (in Arabic), *al-Mustaqbal*, February 2014, accessed 7 June 2017, www.almustaqbal.com/v4/Article.aspx?Type=np&Articleid=604364.

have received disproportionate favours within that system, regardless of whether they belonged to a numerically minor or major group within the social fabric.

Awad's application of the Deleuze/Guattari framework to the Syrian conflict sheds useful light for us on the way ahead for the church, particularly in Muslim contexts, and increasingly globally. If the state of being a numerical minority is different from the process of minoritization, the only way to act is to refuse to accept being a victim. The minority church in majority settings must challenge the minoritization process prophetically, remembering that being a minority is an accident of history that does not make the process of being minoritized inevitable or acceptable.

Based on these definitions of "minority" and "majority" we must work towards a paradigm shift in self-perception as a new starting point for the Middle Eastern church's missional thinking in the context of Islam. If Arab Christians begin to reject this minoritization, they may begin to reintegrate once again as an essential part of the social fabric.

Challenging Minoritization Prophetically

Based on the above, if the church is to act prophetically and missionally in its context, the first step must take place in our minds. Our journey from being victims of minoritization to being simply a factual minority that is positively active in society will need to begin with a paradigm shift in our thinking. We are to reject the process of minoritization imposed on us, not only from outsiders who mean to harm us, but also from those within our own constituencies who mean us well. For indeed, when Christians in the West perceive Arab Christians as minorities who need to be rescued, this victimizes and minoritizes them.

The second step involves our emotions. As long as we feel like victims of our environments, we cannot develop normally, as a confident church redeemed by God and called to be transforming agents in our societies. Yet the hurt that Christians in Muslim lands have experienced throughout history is real. Just as with victims of sexual abuse, if the reality of our hurt is denied, both by our aggressors and by our brothers and sisters within the global church, this will only lead to our feeling twice and thrice spiritually abused and perpetually violated. If the only thing we seek from the global body of Christ is pity, this will obstruct our healing, in the same way as the lack of acknowledgement will obstruct it. The beginning of our healing process needs to take place within our own souls, which only God can touch and heal deeply. Ultimately, the only way for us to find the sort of deep healing in our emotions that releases us for greater things is to create situations that offer our abusers the opportunity to recognize and acknowledge the violence that we have suffered.

The third aspect of change must be in our behaviour. Practically speaking, the church needs to get out of its ghetto mentality. Rather than keeping a low profile, as we have often done, we are called to come back into the public square and not hide behind our fears that have paralysed us. By the grace of God, this has already begun in spite of us, as we have been called to respond to the Syrian refugee crisis. The flow of millions of Syrian refugees throughout the Middle East has shaken the church to its core. By the grace of God, many have responded by praying for those who persecuted us, blessing those who cursed us and loving those who hurt us (Matt 5:44). This has opened wide the gates of heaven with divine blessings.

We begin to challenge minoritization prophetically in our behaviour when we find the strength and rationale to break out of the cycle of violence instituted by a sense of victimhood. Similar to situations of institutionalized racism and prejudice, breaking the cycle of victimhood begins to take place when we find the strength to discern between individual perpetrators and the larger group to which they belong. Our Muslim neighbour today need not be assimilated to Muslim armies and governments that have persecuted Christians in history. Our Muslim neighbour need not be assimilated to Muslims who continue to inflict harm on Christians elsewhere. By differentiating between perpetrators of harm and their larger group, we find enough features in common with our peaceful Muslim neighbours such that perpetrators of violence will themselves become the isolated "minority."

In line with the Deleuze/Guattari hypothesis, we achieve our own de-minoritization when we are able to "connect" and "conjugate" enough "minority elements" – such as moderation, openness, good neighbourliness and loving hospitality – so as to achieve a new "specific, unforeseen, autonomous" majority that works for the common good, in a civil society that seeks justice and equality for all of its members.[10]

The Prophetic Calling of Interfaith Engagement

The evangelical church has historically been a movement of evangelization par excellence. The core features of the movement, as defined by some of its most respected proponents, have been beliefs in the supremacy of the Bible, the

---

10. Deleuze and Guattari, *A Thousand Plateaus*, 106.

majesty of Christ and his sacrificial death, the lordship of the Holy Spirit, the necessity of conversion, the priority of evangelism, the importance of activism and the necessity of communal fellowship.[11] The rejection of one or more of these features, though not necessarily placing its holder outside the fold of Christianity, would nevertheless call into question that person's identification with evangelicalism. Together with a belief in the supreme authority of Scripture and historically orthodox doctrine, a firm belief in mission of word and deed can never be divorced from the evangelical identity.

Increasingly, since about 2007, global evangelicalism has also ventured into the field of interfaith dialogue. One prompt for such consideration was the issuing in 2007 of an open letter by 138 Islamic scholars inviting senior church leaders to meet for dialogue. The letter was addressed to a long list of recipients covering all Christian traditions. The letter and the response to it became known as "A Common Word."[12] Simply put, the letter was an invitation to which there were three possible responses: accept, decline or ignore. Whilst some Christians argued that it was a trap or a cover for more sinister activities, others chose to engage.

Miroslav Volf, Joseph Cumming and others responsible for the "Yale Response to A Common Word," themselves evangelicals, set the tone for this approach in the evangelical world.[13] I myself participated in the 2008 follow-up conference organized by the Yale Center for Faith and Culture and contributed to the ensuing publication.[14] Evangelical Christians are by no means unanimous at this point on interfaith dialogue as a legitimate expression of their mission. But the conviction is on the increase, and once a sufficient number of respected evangelicals have worked out the right balance between vibrant witness and dialogue, it is likely that interfaith dialogue will make it onto the list of accepted evangelical distinctives. I made my initial humble contribution to the conversation by developing the concept of "kerygmatic interaction" in the edited volume of Evelyne Reisacher, *Toward Respectful Understanding*

---

11. See, for example, J. I. Packer, *The Evangelical Anglican Identity Problem* (Oxford: Latimer House, 1978); D. W. Bebbington, *Evangelicalism in Modern Britain* (London: Unwin Hyman, 1989); Alister McGrath, *Evangelicalism and the Future of Christianity* (London: Hodder and Stoughton, 1994); John Stott, *Evangelical Truth* (Leicester: IVP, 1999).

12. See www.acommonword.com/ (accessed 14 November 2017) which lists the senders and recipients together with other information.

13. "'A Common Word' Christian Response," Yale Center for Faith and Culture, accessed 14 November 2017, https://faith.yale.edu/common-word/common-word-christian-response.

14. Miroslav Volf, Prince Ghazi bin Muhammad bin Talal and Melissa Yarrington, eds., *A Common Word: Muslims and Christians on Loving God and Neighbor* (Grand Rapids: Eerdmans, 2009).

and Witness among Muslims. There I described the kerygmatic approach to Christian–Muslim interaction as "devoid of polemical aggressiveness, apologetic defensiveness, existential adaptiveness, or syncretistic elusiveness; not because any of these other four approaches is necessarily wrong, but because that is the nature of the kerygma: God's gracious and positive invitation of humanity into relationship with himself through Jesus. It needs essentially no militant enforcers, no fanatic defenders, no smart adapters, and no crafty revisers."[15]

The term "kerygmatic" is derived from the Greek *kerygma* meaning "proclamation." It is used here as a name for an approach to understanding and participating in Christian–Muslim interaction. The appendix gives a description of five such ways which are identified by their initials as the SEKAP scale.

I believe that the kerygmatic approach to Christian–Muslim interaction is the expression of mission most needed in this age of dramatic conflicts and wars. The church globally cannot simply stand by, either retreating from Islam out of fear or adopting an aggressive attitude that treats all Muslims as belonging to a single homogenous entity. We can no longer afford, as some do, to view the Qur'an simply as an anti-Scripture that we read and understand in a way that is devoid of the sort of sophisticated hermeneutic we require in the reading and interpretation of the Bible. If we are to engage kerygmatically, we must learn the tools of the new trade, learning the method that Muslims use in their approach to the Qur'an, as well as approaching the Qur'an more scientifically and critically, even through the deconstructionist, revisionist lens, but never polemically.

The Church's Ministry as Peacebuilding

The prophetic calling of the church requires that we be responsive to Christ's call to his disciples to be peacebuilders. It is my view that we have taken too lightly Jesus's invitation: "Blessed are the peacemakers, for they will be called children of God" (Matt 5:9). There are not many passages in the Gospels where Jesus identifies his followers as "children of God." The other notable place is where John identifies "those who receive[d] him [Jesus], . . . those who believed in his name," as having been given "the right to become children of God – children born not of natural descent, nor of human decision or a husband's

---

15. Evelyne Reisacher, *Toward Respectful Understanding and Witness among Muslims: Essays in Honor of J. Dudley Woodberry* (Pasadena: William Carey Library, 2015), 38.

will, but born of God" (John 1:12–13). The children of the kingdom are to substitute their perception of being a minority in a hostile environment with the status of being "children of God" who transform society. This is a "minority status" that leaves no room for minoritization.

The apostle Paul understood this calling well when he summarized the mission of the church as the "ministry of reconciliation" (2 Cor 5:18). The cross of Christ justifies us, through faith, achieving for us "peace with God through our Lord Jesus Christ" (Rom 5:1). In a blog post on 4 May 2017,[16] I argued that the New Testament teaching on peace can be understood in its full glory only when read against the background of the Old Testament and its concept of shalom. The messianic expectations prophesied about in the book of Isaiah contain the promise of "a child," "a son," whose "government will be on his shoulders," who will be called the "Prince of Peace," and of whose "government and peace there will be no end" (Isa 9:6–7). The mission of peace inaugurated by this messianic Lord is not one that can be confined within the walls of a church building. It penetrates governments and social realms and will endure for ever. However, from Isaiah to the Gospels, there is also a dramatic realization that the Messiah is called to glory only after his ministry has taken him to the cross and to terrible suffering. For example, "But he was pierced for our transgressions, he was crushed for our iniquities; the punishment that brought us peace was on him, and by his wounds we are healed" (Isa 53:5).

Through the New Testament fulfilment of Isaiah's prophecies, we come to the realization that God's peace does not come cheaply, nor is it enforced through human understandings of power. "By his wounds we are healed" indeed, but then only to be willing in turn to lay down our own lives for our neighbours. The prophetic peacebuilding ministry of the church is no less than an extension of God's self-giving love. It is through this ministry of peacebuilding and reconciliation through the giving of ourselves that we will be recognized as "children of God." Where, then, is our boastful, even aggressive and sometimes violent, discourse about Islam? It has no place among the children of the kingdom.

---

16. Martin Accad, "Biblical Peace Begins at Home: Challenging Common Notions of Peace in the Global Church," IMES blog, 4 May 2017, accessed 14 November 2017, https://imes. blog/2017/05/04/biblical-peace-begins-at-home-challenging-common-notions-of-peace-in-the-global-church/.

The Church's Ministry as Kerygmatic Proclamation

If the ministry of the church is so intrinsically bound to the reconciling ministry of God in Christ, then, through initiatives of peacebuilding, followers of Jesus find themselves at the heart of a ministry of proclamation – the kerygma of the cross. From kerygmatic interaction, we are led to engage in kerygmatic peacebuilding. There are many theories and methodologies of peacebuilding around today. One can obtain university degrees in "peace studies." Many of these have been inspired by giants of our recent history, such as Mahatma Gandhi, Nelson Mandela and Martin Luther King. But what is often overlooked is the extent to which all three were deeply inspired and influenced by the way of Jesus. Kerygmatic peacebuilding, therefore, returns to the Master, by focusing on the self-givingness of the incarnation and the cross, leading to the power and hope of the resurrection. What does our hopeless world, steeped in violence, need more today than the hope of glory found in faith in Christ's resurrection?

The vision of the Arab Baptist Theological Seminary (ABTS) is "to see God glorified, people reconciled, and communities restored through the Church, in the Arab world."[17] Inspired by this vision, ABTS's Institute of Middle East Studies (IMES) has begun to form groups of young Christians and Muslims all over Lebanon to speak together about their faith and how it inspires them to build together a new vision for the common good. Through this *khebz w meleh* (literally, "bread and salt") initiative, we are working to see the emergence of a movement that adheres to Christ's approach to peace. Through it we are building a network of faith leaders all over Lebanon who will work together on impacting their faith communities, and eventually the political elite, in a way that will not leave Lebanon to the mercy and fate of historical accidents. The church in Lebanon is called to play a role of massive transformation through every sphere of society.

Devotional Pause: Psalm 137 (by Gary Nelson)

Psalm 137 asks how God's people can sing their songs in a foreign land. This is the critical question asked by the psalmist in the midst of marginalization, of being in a new location, situation or context which one does not know and where one has few, if any, privileges.

---

17. Vision statement of ABTS, accessed 6 January 2018, https://abtslebanon.org/about/vision-mission/.

Some Western Christians continue to struggle with recognizing the linkages between Christianity and Empire. If Babylon is a metaphor for Empire, we must recognize as Western Christianity that we were Babylon. Our disease is rooted in the loss of our privileged position. Pushed to the margins by secularization, many of us desire to recover the place we once had. Living in a world that we did not choose, we either endeavour to cling onto what once was or we learn to "sing" the song required for the times we are in.

In our sense of loss, like the psalmist in Psalm 137, we imagine a past much better than it really was (Ps 137:4–6). In our worst moments we simply get angry crying for revenge and vengeance (Ps 137:7–9). A process of truth, peace and reconciliation can assist with handling these all-too-human responses. Being clear about the truth of past events, together with lamenting the effects on people at the time and since, is a necessary preparation for constructive, broadly supported actions towards an agreed, shared future.

Peter Drucker, in a public lecture, once noted that, unless the culture changes at the deepest levels, trying to strategize new directions (learning to sing a new song) or creating programs of action will be ineffective. His mantra is "Culture eats strategy for breakfast."[18] Lebanese Christians' general attitudes towards Muslims serve as a great example. The transformation of the Garbage Village in Cairo described in chapter 3 started with changing people's attitudes. Similar examples can be found in Canada, the UK, Rwanda and other countries.

Jeremiah 29:4–9 may very well be God's answer to the question about learning to sing in a foreign land. It starts with changing one's attitude. Through Jeremiah, God tells his people that it is not by chance that they are in Babylon. God put them there.

We live in that reality today. Whether or not we like it, God has placed us where we are and, like the Israelites in exile, we must engage with the society where we are. We must get over whatever is holding us back from getting involved.

---

18. This observation was first made during a lecture and was made more widely known by Mark Fields during his time as President of Ford Motor Company.

Cross-Check: An Active Presence Rooted in a Universal Identity in Christ (by Ehab el-Kharrat)

Our focus moves to Egypt and some insightful comments by Ehab el-Kharrat.

There are three themes to this critical reflection. First, we must behold the human spirit: we must see the image of God in people that is able to put joy on the faces of some in the midst of difficult situations. Second, Christians have an active presence in society, which includes a spirit of witnessing. As discussed in chapter 1, we [Egyptian Christians] do not seek martyrdom but we accept that it has occurred at certain times and is likely to continue to do so. Finally, as Christians we have a universal, eternal and unshakeable identity in Christ.

In 1974 the Lausanne Covenant called on the church to "become a fit instrument in his hands, that the whole earth may hear his voice."[19] It was a call for a three-fold demonstration of the gospel of Jesus based on presence, proclamation and persuasion. We have seen several big changes since that time. The church has a presence everywhere including in many places of work. In terms of specific mission activities, we have become involved in many areas, including education, health, business, sports, politics, media, arts and science. Yet we must beware of thinking that we become the same as everyone else.

In Egypt, Pastor Sammy of Qasr al-Dūbārah Presbyterian Church was a key figure in the shift in thinking throughout the Egyptian church. Scripture reading and Bible study became more widespread. The Orthodox Church did likewise, with their priests preaching from Scripture. Service attendance increased and church buildings became full. There were many conversions to Christ. All church traditions in Egypt became involved. Another trend was increasing pietism within the church. For some, this led to a Noah's ark-type mentality of separation from, and minimal involvement in, "this world."

Our traditional, long-standing ethics included no smoking, no drinking of alcohol and ensuring people were treated fairly at work in terms of pay and conditions. In recent decades, some new ministries have emerged, including working with addicts, the victims of human trafficking and inmates in prison. The church has a much broader and more active presence in society. Yet we need to pray more and offer insightful theological reflections. Both will

---

19. Lausanne Movement, "The Lausanne Covenant," 1 August 1974, accessed 14 November 2017, https://www.lausanne.org/content/covenant/lausanne-covenant, section 14.

keep challenging minoritization and make us more effective "salt and light" (Matt 5:13–16).

In Egypt, Christians were, historically, a minority founded by the apostles who became a majority under the Roman Empire and returned to being a minority at some point following the emergence of Islam. We need to lament that much of the spread of Christianity was due to violent as well as appropriate and godly methods. The social sciences teach us that the Christian response to disease was a significant factor in the rise of Christianity in the second and third centuries. Society rejected the sick, but Christians cared for them despite the risk of being infected. Some Christians had their immunity strengthened, while others became ill and died, a form of martyrdom. As discussed in chapter 1, definitions of martyrdom can be broad. Was there a false sense of infallibility in the motivations of some?

Many terrorist activities are rooted in martyrdom and what appears to be a rather materialistic and worldly concept of reward in heaven. In contrast, many Christians are wary of thinking about eternity. When we do so, our concept of heaven is different, focused on intrinsic, relational values expressed as a community with totally harmonious relationships. We are, and should remain, different.

A broad sweep of Egyptian history in the twentieth century shows a push towards modernity in 1922 and a revolt against modernity in 1989. One barometer/indicator is the prevalence with which the veil is worn by women: photographs of Cairo University in 1960 show very few students wearing veils whereas in 2015 they were common.

One debate among Egyptian Christians is over ethnicity. Some describe themselves as Phoenician (see Glossary), not Arab. They ask whether their ancestors chose to speak Arabic or whether it was imposed on them. But, as Christians, we have a universal identity. Matthew 17:24–27 describes Jesus and Peter at the temple addressing whether or not they should pay the temple tax. Jesus notes that, as children of the Father, of God, they should be exempt. Yet, to maintain good relations with all, they paid the tax using a coin provided by miraculous means. We could say that the Father paid on behalf of his children. We have an identity that is higher than the universe, the cosmos, humanity, nationality by birth or migration, family, tribe, denomination or individual impulses.

Peter and Paul, and Jesus, were proud of their ethnicity and heritage. Yet they saw themselves as part of something larger. Likewise, we need to embrace our heritage but not be restricted by it. Our sense of identity is rooted in Christ. This should enable us to identify with everyone everywhere, to maintain a cosmic awareness of the purposes and actions of our God. The whole of creation needs to be seen in the presence and purposes of God. Yet the world is a collection of particularities. These matter; they have significance to us and to others. We must not wipe them out or pretend that they do not matter. But we do need to maintain our vision of a larger, wider, richer and deeper sense of identity in Christ and of being part of God's plans and purposes. When Jesus saw the faith of the centurion as described in Matthew 8:5–13 he saw beyond "covenant people" as ethnically defined.

Part of the present heritage of Christians in Egypt and elsewhere is being minoritized. As Ramez Atallah remarked in chapter 1, we need to recall that Egypt's national heritage includes being Christian before becoming Muslim. It also includes the pre-Christian history, which profoundly affects Egypt as well as other parts of the Middle East.

We [Middle Eastern Christians] have to take our message outside our church buildings and Christian communities to everyone. This requires rising above minoritization, refusing to accept the constraints that others seek to impose on us.

We move to stories of two Christians seeking to respond to being minoritized. The first takes us to Iraq before we return to Lebanon, thereby completing a circular tour of part of the Middle East. Both stories have elements of ethnic as well as religious identity.

Witness 1: Haitham – The Changing Nature of the Church in Iraq

Pastor Haitham Jazrawi lives and works in Kirkuk, Iraq. He regards himself as part of a minority within a minority, numerically, since evangelical Christians are a small part of the Christian community in which the Assyrians, Armenians and Chalcedonians (see Glossary) are large groups. Historically, these large groups are the native peoples of the area, in so far as their sense of religious identity predates that of the Shi'a and Sunni communities.

The religious identity of Christians in Iraq is recognized legally. In addition, they have an ethnic identity, as do their fellow Iraqis. Society, though, does limit how people are allowed to describe themselves. This creates identity challenges for some. There are Iraqis who care more about ethnicity than about their religious heritage, including some, but by no means all, Christians.

Developments in Iraq since 2014 have included calls to close seven church buildings on the grounds that there are no Christians nearby to worship in them. One is in Baghdad, one in Mosul has been destroyed by ISIS and one case will be problematic because the land has been taken and allocated for another purpose by the authorities. Pastor Haitham is one church leader who would like Christians to return to reopen church buildings.

Pastor Haitham's question is whether Christians, especially evangelicals, will return. In his city of Kirkuk there are big church buildings. His desire is for Christians to act as yeast because of who they are (Matt 13:33).

Witness 2: Elias – Palestinian and Christian in Lebanon

Elias Habib lives in Lebanon. Ethnically, he is Palestinian and religiously he is a Christian. He lives in a Palestinian refugee camp. There are eleven such camps in Lebanon, only one of which has a recognized Christian presence, Dbayeh. His camp has very poor housing conditions with few public services and no school.

Palestinian Christians are doubly vulnerable. Some have been told by fellow Christians that "your Christ is different from our Christ." A further problem within Elias's situation is that a few church leaders speak on behalf of this community when they are distant from it. Accordingly, these self-appointed spokesmen have no legitimacy in the eyes of those they claim to be representing. Many clerics are remote from their people, unable to live in the communities where most of their congregations reside. Consequently, they can provide limited support and can appear to lack compassion. This exacerbates minoritization by denying people a voice and authentic representation. Elias's preference would be that they enable the people of the camp to speak for themselves.

One specific challenge is graveyards. Those that exist are being maintained by the community. Inevitably, over time the graveyards have become full. Land is very limited for the Palestinian community which has been told by the Lebanese authorities that no more space can be made available. The injunction to bury people in Palestine is impossible to implement, much as many Palestinians might wish to do so. This is a very troubling topic for the Palestinian community in Lebanon: it reminds them that they have no access to their ancestral homeland and have, at best, a limited welcome in Lebanon.

How should we respond to the lack of a school, a place for burials and a recognized local voice, and to being doubly disadvantaged? What would Elias like most of all? In the short term, he would like a school to be provided for the camp's residents; in the longer term, that the roots of the double humiliation be addressed. This is a call for greater acceptance and integration of the Palestinian diaspora within Lebanese society which, in turn, is part of the wider injustice of the situation of Palestinians throughout the Middle East, as discussed by Daniel Bannoura and Yohanna Katanacho in the three previous chapters.

Global Cross-Check: France's Evangelical Christian Community (by Philip Halliday)

> *Christians being a minority in society is not restricted to the Middle East. Throughout Europe, Christians, measured as those who attend churches regularly, are a minority, well below half of the population. Many feel that they are marginalized. To what extent are they minoritized? Our consideration of such questions is led by Philip Halliday, a British church leader who has lived and worked in France for many years.*

When you think of France, what images come into your mind? A pavement café, a château on the Loire River or the Eiffel Tower? Or perhaps the bread, cheese, wine and other elements of French cuisine? How well do we remember photographs from 2005 entitled "France on fire," when many thousands of cars were set on fire in cities all over the country?

France can be regarded as the Islamic capital of Europe, with about 10 percent of the population being Muslim. France is believed to have the highest number of converts to Islam within Europe, although reliable figures are impossible to obtain. However, French Muslims' political and social presence within society does not match their numbers: one can observe a growing frustration with cultural and religious marginalization and discrimination in French society. And yet it is precisely the expression of this frustration that leads the population to regularly conclude that religion, and religious people, are a source of trouble and that France would be better off without them.

France's rather fierce secularism is part of the country's identity and integral to its history. The French did not simply "lose track" of their Christian heritage: they consciously rejected it; the Republic won out over the conservative Catholicism associated with an oppressive past. Today, the secularism in France is determined and articulate, with the population defending itself against religion and religious people.

For more than 100 years, France has been a secular country in which no church or religion has been recognized by the state but in which everyone has had the right to worship freely. Most Protestants in France welcomed the separation of church and state as being the achievement of religious freedom after centuries of Catholic domination. However, one consequence is that, since the separation in 1905, teaching religion in French schools has not been allowed. In 2016 a child was sent home from her school's Christmas party because she arrived wearing an angel costume which was deemed to violate the principle of "no religious symbols."

Moreover, previous generations of Catholics were mainly taught Catholic principles and tradition rather than the Bible. Consequently, in 2017 there is a deep ignorance about the Christian faith and about Christians. Less than 5 percent of the population attend any church on a weekly basis. The Bible is pretty much a closed book, with a recent survey revealing that three out of four French people have never opened a Bible. As is often the case, ignorance produces fear and suspicion.

As a church leader in the UK, it seemed to me perfectly normal for there to be a choice of churches in every town. I took it for granted that even those who did not attend were usually glad, nonetheless, that those churches were there. Indeed, it was because I [Philip Halliday] was a minister that I was invited into schools, youth clubs, hospitals, retirement homes, and so on. Even those parents who never came to church themselves were happy to entrust their children to us when the church provided a holiday club or a Sunday school outing.

When I arrived in France, it was a very different story. Evangelical Christians are usually gathered in small congregations and generally spread out – tens of miles – from one another. Parents protect their children from religious people, wary of what their intentions might be. Somewhat anxious and suspicious, they prefer to keep even evangelical Christians at a distance.

Returning to France's state secularism, there are some anomalies. First, the French state owns a number of church buildings and religious monuments. Second, some confessional schools, particularly Roman Catholic, are mainly financed by the state to educate the nation's children while maintaining their religious confessions. Third, the French regions of Alsace and Lorraine used to be part of Germany and, because of that, are governed by different rules in matters of religion. For example, Roman Catholic priests, certain Protestant pastors (Reformed and Lutheran) and Jewish rabbis are paid by the state – financed by a local religious tax – and these faiths are taught in schools. Will these arrangements extend to Islam in the future? Will Islam be taught in school and will the imams be paid by the state in these two regions of France?

Prior to the Second World War (1939–45), the French government used the word "neutral" (*neutralité*) to describe its position on religion. The word "secular" (*laïcité*) entered the vocabulary in 1948, when there was a unanimous vote in parliament.

Until around 1980, the secularism was fairly low-key and easy-going. Secularism was understood correctly: not as an alternative to religion but rather as a framework in which both the religious and non-religious could function.

But the climate changed around 1980 and tensions began to increase. I believe that the change was due to the growth of Islam and to the growth of evangelicalism. I suggest there has been an atmosphere of concern and suspicion about people of faith.

In Europe at large, the state's secular position does not prevent it from dialoguing with religious people and, to some extent, working with them. In France, however, since about 1980, that has not been the case. Rather, the state's attitude has been one of abstention and suspicion. I would suggest that the neutrality of the state in France – to use the old word – has been partially lost and there is now some prejudice against religious people.

In summer 2016 women were banned from wearing the full-body swimsuit or "burkini" and they were fined if they did wear one. What is the difference between a burkini and a wetsuit? And what about Catholic nuns who go for a swim wearing a habit? There are very few differences between habits, wetsuits and burkinis when assessed purely as articles of clothing.

There are examples of prejudice against evangelical Christians. One is that churches sometimes find it hard to get building permission from their local government, or their requests to buy land are rejected. Another example concerns when the government helps pay for poorer families to go on a holiday. This money is regularly withheld if the family wants to go on holiday with a Christian organization – even when that organization has the correct paperwork and government approval for its safety measures and the competence of its leaders. A third example is complaints in the local press whenever a town hall lends churches some sound equipment.

Added to the prejudice from the French state, there would seem to be some confusion among the French population about what it means to be a secular country. We remarked earlier that secularism – correctly understood – is not an alternative to religion but rather is a neutral framework in which the religious and non-religious can function. Secularism is the guarantee of the freedom of religion and belief for all. However, you regularly hear the argument – particularly at times of social unrest – that, as a secular country, France ought to ban all religions.

The adoption of anti-sect legislation since 2001 has been, in some senses, an attempt for the state to once again define what is a "good" religion and what is "bad"' or "toxic" religion. In recent years, for example, there have been periods when the Protestant Federation of France has come under political pressure to expel the evangelicals and to limit its membership to those who are thought of as being the more "mainstream" Protestants, such as Reformed and Lutherans. This is a worrying development and one that threatens the religious freedom that evangelicals have enjoyed in France for more than 100 years.

Most of the practising Protestants in France are evangelical (67 percent) but, nonetheless, all these evangelical Christians represent less than 1 percent of the French population. If you count all the Protestant evangelicals together, they have just 2,014 churches throughout the country. This compares with more than 2,600 Baptist congregations in the UK, a country with roughly the same population as France. It goes without saying that evangelicals are not widely known. Indeed, even serious journalists commonly make the mistake of calling them "evangelists" (*évangélistes*) rather than "evangelicals" (*évangéliques*). A link is frequently made between evangelicalism and Pentecostalism or between evangelicalism and fundamentalism. The assumption is often made that evangelicalism must be a foreign import, probably from America – which is not a good recommendation as far as the French are concerned!

Nevertheless, the number of French evangelicals has multiplied nine-fold since 1957. Some of them are part of what many refer to as the "historical church," with roots that go back to the sixteenth-century Reformation. As such, they are members of the French Protestant Federation, as we noted above. Other evangelicals, however, are not. In order to bring these two groups together, the National Council of French Evangelicals was created in 2010. It brings together thirty different evangelical denominations, plus a number of para-church organizations. It includes Pentecostal and charismatic groups, on the one hand, and much more conservative groups, on the other.

This National Council of French Evangelicals aims to encourage unity and collaboration between the various evangelical groups but also to provide a national voice for them. It is significant that the President of this Council was invited to the investiture ceremony of Emmanuel Macron as President of France on 14 May 2017.

Positively, the National Council of French Evangelicals has united a broad range of diverse churches with the goal of planting one evangelical congregation for every 10,000 people in France. But alongside these very positive goals, there is a need to represent *and* protect the interests of the French evangelical minority in the public square. As noted in chapter 1, the public square ought to be a noisy and creative space, welcoming the expression of the views of all those who seek to do no harm.

A Canadian Perspective: The Treatment of the Original Inhabitants (by Gary Nelson)

Gary Nelson points out that Canadian history contains a festering wound: the treatment of the original inhabitants. This group of people were very minoritized.

From the 1880s to late in the twentieth century a number of government programs placed all those under eighteen in boarding schools, well away from their families and communities. The intention was to remove their original culture. It was social engineering applied to a whole ethnic group. I note that the church was part of such initiatives, a fact that I regard as shameful.

Two developments in recent years have sought to address this legacy. One was a series of "truth and reconciliation" meetings. The other is the development of an MA in Aboriginal Peoples which is fully taught by such people. This is offered by Tyndale University College and Seminary in partnership with an NGO. This is the church explicitly working to bring healing and reconciliation, and to facilitate these people being able to flourish on their own terms.

Similar social engineering schemes were perpetrated on indigenous peoples in other countries. One trusts that people of goodwill are endeavouring to address such situations.

Leading Prophetically

In this chapter we have described why minoritization must be resisted and have described several approaches for doing so. As with the subjects discussed in previous chapters, one-size-fits-all solutions are unlikely to be found in disorienting times. However, common elements of resistance and rejection will include consideration of our own thinking and emotions: we need to be clear about who we are in Christ.

As a global church, we need to be aware that minoritization can occur anywhere; no community is immune, irrespective of its history. Each generation must be faithful in witness, testimony and passing on the faith. As a global church, we need to hear the clear request of those in the Middle East to be very careful about how we describe their context and how we stand alongside them. They do not seek protection or rescue: these harm them more than support them. Neither do they desire to be referred to as a minority, a request that (perhaps) applies worldwide. They need prayerful encouragement to be faithful to who God made them, and all Christians, to be. Two Syrian contributors noted that numbers are not in themselves significant. What is crucial is Christians being proactively engaged with the societies that they are part of, seeking to bring transformation to as many communities as possible.

Christians within the Middle East are evaluating how they relate to and interact with their Muslim neighbours. We have noted the vast diversity among Muslims, theologically and in how they seek to express their faith in the public square. This chapter has emphasized a kerygmatic approach, one that is Christ-centred, prayerful and clear about witness whilst being respectful and attentive to the views of those of other faiths. The public square needs the presence of Christians willing and able to contribute. This applies at local, municipal, national and international levels. It can be viewed as an injunction to engagement in society in response to the message of Scripture and the call of God on individuals and fellowships.

Questions for Reflection

1. The early church were oppressed, misunderstood, had no worldly power but did not see themselves as powerless; instead, they saw themselves as the beloved of God, giving them a very strong identity in Christ. How can we recover this mindset? How can we express it?

2. In societies that we know well, who is marginalized and who is minoritized? How can we stand alongside them? How can we enable them to resist being so treated?

3. How can we become better peacemakers? And how does that relate to our pursuit of justice for all, our dialogue with those of other faiths and our kerygmatic proclamation?

Conclusion

We have asked how one can live in confusing, chaotic, dynamic, disorienting circumstances. One answer is found in Jeremiah 29, where God tells his people what their attitude should be: to recognize that he has put them where they are. Therefore, they should get involved in society; if it prospers, so will they. Be productive, contributing members of communities and nations. Consequently, whatever we think of our circumstances, they are what God has given us for now.

This is a "big picture" approach to living in disorienting times, in an era when the pace of change frequently feels faster than the pace of learning, which necessitates managing a sense of inadequacy or failure.

We have examined four themes: persecution and suffering, emigration, hopelessness and despair, and minoritization. In some senses, the fourth, minoritization, is a composition of the previous three. This chapter called on Christians across the Middle East and North Africa to recognize when they are being minoritized – that is, being overtly oppressed – and to respond by resisting being so treated in both attitude and action. Christians should be who God made them to be, secure in their identity in Christ and active citizens within society as a whole. Any attempts to restrict Christians to their own communities should be politely and persistently resisted. Relationships with Muslims as people and Islam as a religion should be defined by a kerygmatic approach that combines clear, respectful witness to Jesus with attentive listening to the views of others.

Will this be easy to live out? Perhaps not, as the first three chapters showed. Yet we have described examples of Christians bringing transformation to the lives of many amidst religious persecution and the general suffering imposed by outside forces and by the internal dynamics of corruption and nepotism.

Jesus warned his followers to expect persecution. This is the reality for many Christians in the Middle East and North Africa. The forms vary by location, including within many countries. For a few, emigration is the only viable option. For most, though, there are options to remain, to be faithful witnesses and to model the love and life that Jesus brings to those who follow him.

As Christians, we follow a God of justice and regard pursuing justice for the whole of society as part of what God expects us, collectively, to do. An analysis of systems and structures that perpetrate and perpetuate injustice within society is an essential element of seeking transformation. We do not critique systems of Empire simply to deconstruct the present: we seek a changed, transformed reality for all. How this is expressed will vary by context, especially to the holders of dictatorial powers at local, municipal, national and supra-national levels. In some places, it is possible, both discreetly and overtly in the public square. Elsewhere it is not possible, certainly not in the public square; anyone so doing would be severely minoritized. One example is Syria, as articulated in chapter 3 and analysed in chapter 4. In disorienting times, the dynamics of what is possible where are in a state of flux.

The public square ought to be a vibrant and noisy space, one in which Christians contribute along with adherents of other faiths and none. Christians should be contributors and encourage other communities to also be present. This is a prerequisite for a healthy society.

We have discussed the power of forgiveness, noting examples from Egypt that spoke powerfully to those of other religious beliefs. We have seen an Egyptian television news anchor remark that Egyptian Christians "are made of steel." Offering forgiveness includes an expression that harm has been done, that injustice has been perpetrated. It is not appeasement. It should be seen as part of our pursuit of justice and the restoration of healthy relationships among human beings, all of whom have equal worth and value before God.

Linked to forgiveness is our desire to bring healing and wholeness to all. One aspect of this is radical hospitality which treats strangers, aliens and those who seek to harm us – our enemies – as if they were our brothers or sisters. This is what we should offer as Christ's followers to all who will engage with us.

Emigration continues to be a major challenge, not least because it appears that it is often Christian leaders who have more opportunities to leave than other Christians. We observed that it is meaningless for Christians to stay in the region merely for the sake of staying. The motivation needs to include being the "salt and light" that Jesus calls his followers to be. Christians, like all humans, need to find meaning in life, a sense of purpose that enables them to endure distress and disorientation. Our faith should be a major asset in doing so, in giving a strong sense of calling, of something that God has asked us to do on his behalf. We need to keep in mind that we are participants in God's mission, the *missio Dei*: it remains his, not ours, and never mine. We emphasized that, in seeking God's call, there must be collective as well as individual elements within the discernment process: we need one another, especially in disorienting times.

We critiqued the thinking of "open" and "closed" doors as an aspect of God's guidance and call. One weakness of such thinking is that some Christians have far more connections and hence opportunities than others. We have noted examples of people regarding what others label a "closed door" as an obstacle that must be overcome: such people pursue fulfilling their sense of God's call with persistent determination.

Linked to a sense of calling is a clear sense of identity. As Christians, our identity needs to be rooted first and foremost in our faith, of being "in Christ." Other aspects must be secondary, including gender, marital status, ethnicity, nationality and profession. Such security of identity should enable us to dialogue with anyone. Consequently, we can engage with those who are different, including those who regard us as enemies. As people who have experienced the forgiveness of God, we can be forgiving people.

Hopelessness and despair is the daily reality of all too many. One consequence is an inability to imagine or dream that life can be different and one day will be different. We know that this world is not the way that God intended it to be, nor as he desires that it should be, which should inspire us to work for change, for transformation. We should be leading prophetically, as our Christian faith should enable us to be more imaginative, for ourselves, our communities and for others. We should be articulating in words and demonstrating with persistent presence and actions among those in despair what a transformed society could look like. We should be aware that our societies and nations need us to do so and will benefit from the transformation that we seek to instigate. We should act as if the opposite of hope is a lack of imagination, in the sense that we should be enabling the disadvantaged to dream of a future different from their present circumstances and should stand alongside them as they begin to transform their situation.

One approach is to think of Hope as having two parents, Love and Faith, and two daughters, Anger and Courage: anger at injustice, at the sight of anyone made in the image of God being treated as inferior to others; and the courage to do what we are able to do – ideally, rectify the injustice, and in all cases, mitigate some of the effects thereof. What enables us to do so is the fact that our hope comes from our God. Hence, Hope's parents are Faith and Love: faith in God and recognition that it is love that unites us to God.

Middle Eastern Christians have seen that numbers, religious demographics, are, at best, of secondary importance. More significant is the value of faith in God, expressing itself in persistent, consistent participation in society.

Change often takes time, and can emerge from unlikely sources. This book describes several situations that many would describe as hopeless, yet they have been transformed over time by the faithful, persistent engagement of Christians. The necessity to be committed for years, decades and generations is one element of many such stories. Our expression of hope leads, over time, to the development of relationships built on trust.

In disorienting times, one must question whether there can be such a thing as a comfort zone for a Christian believer. Any such thoughts and feelings of comfort are likely to be disrupted and severely challenged at some point. This reminds us that our identity must be firmly secured in our faith, in our being "in Christ"; anything else will be severely shaken during disorienting times.

One message from the Middle Eastern church to those of us who are members of the Western church is that those who attempt to "protect" them from outside the region are causing as much harm as those in the region who are attempting to oppress them. This is a strong statement. The perception that people need protection from outside distances them and makes them vulnerable within the countries of which they are a part: societies that they are endeavouring to influence.

A second message to Western Christians is not to encourage Middle Eastern church leaders to emigrate. Stop offering them jobs in the West. Instead, find imaginative ways to stand alongside them, encouraging them to be faithful to their calling, their fellow Christians and to their families. The flipside of this is to encourage those of Middle Eastern origin resident in the West to explore a sense of God's call on their lives, whether that means they remain in the West or return to the lands of their ancestry.

Some ask what the future of the Middle East without its Christians might be. For us, it is better to transpose this question to one about the future of the church. For the Middle Eastern church, disorienting times are an opportunity to be seen as an integral part of the region, working for transformation at local and national levels for the benefit of all. The only people who want to see all Christians leave are some of the violent jihadists. Everyone else, including some we might term as Islamists, desires their continued presence. They recognize that it is Christians who are the leaven that permeates the whole of society.

In the face of minoritization, Christians need to forge a theology of witness and martyrdom. The latter is never to be sought, but nor is it to be unduly feared. Christians have a solid doctrine of assurance: our eternal future has been secured by Jesus Christ. The church throughout the Middle East seeks to remain present in the region, to be faithful in witness and testimony, and an active agent of transformation. Whenever martyrdom occurs, the response should be one of noting injustice, of calling for justice, of pronouncing forgiveness and of the proclamation, the *kerygma*, of the good news.

One observation that was made is that God usually does great things only through those who have been greatly broken. This encourages us when we face difficult times and when we stand alongside others in dark places, especially those enduring persecution or intense suffering, those feeling hopelessness and despair, and those who have been minoritized. God longs to transform, to bring good things out of bad. This does not in itself make difficulties desirable, although it is perhaps one step on the road to imagining a future different from the present. The move from hopelessness to hope frequently takes time. We need to be people who persist alongside others and who are thankful to God whenever we see transformation occur, be it for an individual, a family, a small group or a suburb of a major city.

Dare we hope for transformation of the Middle East?

Appendix

The Kerygmatic Approach within the SEKAP Scale

The SEKAP scale contrasts five different approaches that various Christians take when engaging with those of other faiths. In our context, we will restrict this to contact with Muslims.

In summary, the one-word titles for the five approaches are syncretistic, existential, kerygmatic, apologetic and polemical. The initial letters give the name of the scale, SEKAP. In practice, most Christians use elements of four of these approaches at different times, the exception being the first. We will discuss each in turn, working from both ends towards the centre so that we conclude with the kerygmatic approach which was endorsed in chapter 4.

The *syncretistic* approach accepts that all religions have part of the truth and everyone may pick the elements of each that they want. To participate in such exchanges, participants do not require a profound understanding of Islam. Critiques of this approach note that all major religions make exclusive truth claims which are mutually incompatible. This undermines the approach from an academic perspective: it denies what all major faiths claim about themselves.

It does, though, occur in practice. For example, on 6 January 2017 a Muslim was invited to read a passage from the Qur'an during a service in Glasgow Cathedral, UK. The speaker read several verses more than the assigned passage in Sura (chapter) 19, entitled Maryan (Mary), with the additional element including a Qur'anic counter-claim to the cross (vv. 35 and 36). This proved controversial. Many regarded the service as syncretistic; some thought it outrageous, including the dean of the cathedral, the senior priest, who resigned in order to express his criticism in public.

Switching to the last element of the SEKAP scale, the *polemical* approach: the word "polemic" is derived from the Greek word *polemos*, meaning war, combat, conflict. The polemical approach is based on argument seeking to show the weaknesses and shortcomings within Islam when contrasted with Christianity. The polemical approach requires detailed knowledge of Islam. It is grounded in the view that all non-Christian religions are invalid and, typically, it treats Islam as a deception.

Some proponents of the polemical approach end up being purely argumentative; their goal becomes to win arguments. This is not praiseworthy! Others state that their objective is to give Muslims a clear understanding of the truth of Christianity and then respect whatever religious choices they make.

One aspect we can note is that Islam has an innately polemical approach towards Christianity since the Qur'an at several points directly contradicts orthodox Christian teaching. We noted an example of this above.

The *existential* approach accepts that all religions promote a sense of morality and consequently there are things in all other religions with which Christians can agree. This approach focuses on finding such common ground and reinforcing inter-communal acceptance and mutual respect. Christians engaging with Muslims need an awareness of Islam's broad outlines.

Some Western religious education curricula within state schools take this approach. The UK is an example.

The *apologetic* approach focuses on explaining Christianity to anyone interested enough to ask. It seeks to demonstrate the truth of Christianity. In discussion with Muslims, this includes responding to the misrepresentation of some Christian beliefs contained in the Qur'an; for example, the view that the Trinity is the Father, Jesus and Mary.

An underlying assumption is the rational view that the exclusive truth claims of the major religions are incompatible, implying that at most one is correct in its understanding of the ultimate realities sustaining the universe.

In the kerygmatic approach, the word "kerygmatic" is derived from the Greek *kerygma*, meaning proclamation. This approach is focused on proclamation of the gospel of Jesus Christ as a whole with the messenger being part of the process due to the indwelling presence of God. This approach is respectful and loving of Muslims. Some describe it as an attitude whose practical expression will include using existential, apologetic and polemic elements as appropriate. Those following this approach endeavour to be prayerfully Christ-centred, intentional about witness and ready to share the hope that lives in them.

Paul uses the word *kerygma* in 1 Corinthians 2:4 and 2 Timothy 4:17. The latter use occurs in the context of having used *apologia* in the previous verse. He was speaking about a court appearance, noting that nobody assisted in his defence, but he was enabled by God to proclaim the message of Jesus.

As we live in the communities of which we are a part, so we should seek out opportunities to be engaged with those of other faiths or none. We must keep in mind that, as people known to be adherents of a religious belief, we are being watched and observed. We should be available to talk about our faith, the hope within us, at all times.

We noted in chapter 1 that the public square should be an open, noisy, colourful, dynamic yet safe space in which Christians, together with adherents of other religions, can express their beliefs. This will always involve challenges, since the exclusive truth claims made by all major religions will be challenged and contested.

Glossary

Alawite an ethnic-religious group accepted as a strand within Shi'a Islam (see below) by some and treated as a distinct religion by others; present in Lebanon, Syria and Turkey

Al-Azhar the leading academic institution within Sunni Islam (see below); located in Cairo, Egypt; the head of al-Azhar also holds the post of Grand Mufti (i.e. senior Muslim cleric) of Egypt

Al-Qaeda a network of armed groups generally subscribing to a similar jihadist (see below) ideology

Arab Spring a socio-political phenomenon that arose in 2011 affecting most countries in the Middle East, North Africa and the Arabian Peninsula typified by protests calling for reform of governance structures, greater opportunity for all and recognition of the dignity and worth of all citizens; referred to as the Arab Awakening and Arab Revolutions by some

Arab world those countries located in the Middle East, North Africa and the Arabian Peninsula where Arabic is a national language (and the mother tongue of many citizens); namely Algeria, Bahrain, Egypt, Iraq, Jordan, Kuwait, Lebanon, Libya, Mauritania, Morocco, Oman, Qatar, Palestine, Saudi Arabia, Sudan, Syria, Tunisia, United Arab Emirates (UAE) and Yemen; many citizens of these countries are not ethnically Arab, e.g. the Kurds, Druze and the various Berber peoples across North Africa; the term "Arab world" can suggest a uniformity when the reality is diversity among these nineteen states

Armenians an ethnic group present in several countries across the Middle East; historically the first ethnic group to collectively become Christians

Assyrians a religious group within Christianity identified by its worship style; seen by some as ethnically distinct

Babylon used in the Bible to mean an imperial, dominating power; one example is 1 Peter 5:13; derived from the Israelites being exiled to the city of Babylon as recorded in the Old Testament

Bedouin a nomadic people group found in many countries throughout the MENA region

Central Asia usually understood as a collective term for Kazakhstan, Kyrgyzstan, Tajikistan, Turkmenistan and Uzbekistan; these are all former Soviet states; some usages include Afghanistan, which was not part of the Soviet Republic

Chalcedonians a strand within Christianity adhering to the doctrines concerning the person of Jesus Christ adopted at the Council of Chalcedon in 451

Christian Zionism a strand within Christian theology that emphasizes the State of Israel as being intrinsically significant to eschatology (i.e. end times); also used in various political circles to indicate unconditional and often uncritical support for the Israeli government (see Zionism below)

Civil Rights Movement political campaign calling for the equality before the law of all citizens; in USA in 1960s the focus was on the rights of African Americans

Daesh the name used by many political and religious leaders in the Middle East for ISIS (see below); it is derived from an approximate acronym of the group's name in Arabic

Druze an ethnic religious group present in Israel, Lebanon and Syria; viewed as a strand within Islam by some and as a distinct religion by others

Empire used here to refer to a political entity acting in dictatorial and often unaccountable ways usually supressing – minoritizing (see chapter 4) – all those who disagree with its policies and actions

Green Line the boundary between Israel and the West Bank that was in operation from 1949 to the Six-Day War in June 1967; it ran through Jerusalem, creating the terms West Jerusalem (part of Israel) and East Jerusalem (part of the West Bank)

Gulf States the small countries of the Arabian Peninsula, usually taken to mean Kuwait, Bahrain, Qatar and the UAE; in some contexts, it includes Oman

Hadith sayings of the prophet Mohammad; there is much debate within Islamic theological circles about the validity of many of them since the historical evidence linking them to the prophet is questionable

Health and wealth the view that God wants his followers to be healthy and rich; discredited by many Christian theologians; some note that this is a very human desire, and versions of such thinking occur in most major religions

ISIS, ISIL an armed group that arose in Iraq around 2006 before re-emerging in Syria in late 2011 or 2012; the group's original official title was The Islamic State of Iraq and ash-Sham; it is referred to as The Islamic State in Iraq and Syria (ISIS) and The Islamic State in Iraq and the Levant (ISIL) in some sources because the Arabic phrase *Belad As-Sham* can refer to Syria and also the entire Levant (see below); the group re-titled itself The Islamic State in July 2014; the term Daesh (see above) is used by some in the Middle East

Islamic world countries whose citizens are mostly adherents of Islam; much broader than the Arab world (see above); most are members of the Organization of Islamic Cooperation (OIC), whose head office is in Jeddah, Saudi Arabia; an exception within the Arab world is Qatar which is not a member of the OIC

Islamist someone seeking to bring about a system of governance derived exclusively from Islamic principles; there is a diversity of views on what a truly Islamic form of governance would be; the methods applied to achieve the goal vary

Jihadist an Islamist willing to use violent means; all jihadists are Islamists, but not all Islamists are jihadists

Kurd an ethnic group with significant numbers in Iran, Iraq, Syria and Turkey; commonly regarded as the largest ethnic group in the world without a state; there are seven distinct Kurdish dialects; most are adherents of Sunni Islam

Levant literally, the lands around Damascus; typically understood to mean modern-day Iraq, Jordan, Lebanon and Syria; some usages include Israel, the West Bank and the Gaza Strip

Logotherapy considered to be the third Viennese School of psychotherapy; it focuses on the "will to find meaning"; contrasts with psychoanalysis, the "will to find pleasure," and individual psychology, the "will to acquire or maintain power"[1]

Muslim Brotherhood a movement within Sunni Islam with religious and political dimensions seeking the establishment of Islamic governance; founded in Egypt; has branches in many countries, some of which use alternative names; all are Islamist but few are jihadist (see above)

Nakba Arabic term used by Palestinians to describe the displacement of Palestinians between 1947 and 1949 inclusive, a period that included the declaration of the State of Israel; literally, "catastrophe"; spelled (or transliterated) Nakbah in some sources

Nineveh Plain geographic area of Iraq close to the city of Mosul and bordering the Kurdish Regional Government administered provinces of Arbil and Dohuk

Oral divorce the practice in some schools of Islamic Shari'a (see below) that allows a man to divorce his wife using a simple, verbal formula

Phoenician a term used by some Egyptian Christians to describe their ethnicity; a mark of being distinct from Arabs

Roma an ethnic group that prefers to live a semi-nomadic lifestyle in Europe; widely dispersed across much of Europe, originally from the Balkans area; referred to as Gypsies by some

Septuagint translation of the Hebrew Scriptures into Greek; it is the edition of the Old Testament most frequently quoted in the New Testament

Shari'a Islamic jurisprudence or law; in its broadest understanding this covers all aspects of life including the daily prayer times as well as matters of criminal, civil and personal status law; there are a variety of interpretations of Shari'a which have been codified giving five Medhabs or schools of Shari'a, one within Shi'a Islam, the Ja'afari school, and four within Sunni Islam, namely the Hanafi, Hanbali, Maliki and Shafi'i schools

Shi'a a strand within Islam; the major groupings within Shi'a Islam are the Ja'afari (also known as the Twelver), the Ismaili (sometimes called the Sevener) and the Zaidi (sometimes referred to as the Fiver) which is closer in many respects to Sunni Islam than other forms of Shi'a Islam

Sufis adherents of a strand within Islam that emphasizes purity of worship and inward mystical experiences of Islam; occurs within both Sunni and Shi'a Islam; often involves an ascetic lifestyle

Sunni a strand within Islam; numerically, the largest broad strand; has several sub-strands

---

1. See Viktor Frankl Institute of Logotherapy, accessed 13 February 2018, www.logotherapyinstitute.org/About_Logotherapy.html.

Talmud a revered text within Judaism, with some ascribing it sacred text status; originates from the writing down of traditional rabbinic teaching; there are various views within Judaism as to which historic texts constitute the Talmud

Theodicy theology of why God allows suffering

UNHCR the United Nations High Commission for Refugees; also referred to as the UN Refugee Agency

Wahhabi a form of Sunni Islam based on the teachings of Mohammad ibn 'Abd al-Wahhab (1703–1792)[2]

Wasta influence; the practice in much of the Middle East (and elsewhere) that one requires influence to gain favour with officials, employers, etc.

West Bank the area east of the Green Line (see above) and west of the River Jordan; the widely accepted border with the State of Israel from 1948 to June 1967; other definitions are used by some, typically excluding East Jerusalem (see Daniel Bannoura's contribution in chapter 1)

Yezidis a Kurdish community (see above) whose distinct monotheistic religious beliefs are derived from Zoroastrianism and ancient Mesopotamian religions; most are located in northern Iraq with small numbers in Syria and among Kurdish diasporas

Zionism a nationalistic movement about a state for the Jewish people in the historic land of Israel; prior to 1948, Zionism focused on the establishment of such a state; since 1948, it has focused on the continued existence and security of the nation-state of Israel (see Christian Zionism above)

---

2. See "Islamic Radicalism: Its Roots and Current Representation," The Islamic Supreme Council of America, accessed 7 November 2017, www.islamicsupremecouncil.org/understanding-islam/anti-extremism/7-islamic-radicalism-its-wahhabi-rootsand-current-representation.html.

Bibliography

Alexander, Paul ed. *Christ at the Checkpoint: Theology in the Service of Justice and Peace*. Eugene: Wipf & Stock, 2012.

Andrews, Jonathan. *Identity Crisis: Religious Registration in the Middle East*. Malton: Gilead, 2016.

————. *Last Resort: Migration and the Middle East*. Malton: Gilead, 2017.

Barreto, Raimundo C. Jr., Ken Sehested, and Luis Rivera-Pagán, eds. *Engaging the Jubilee: Freedom and Justice Papers of the Baptist World Alliance (2010–2015)*. Falls Church, VA: Baptist World Alliance, 2015.

Bebbington, D. W. *Evangelicalism in Modern Britain*. London: Unwin Hyman, 1989.

Berlin, Adele. *Lamentations*. The Old Testament Library. Louisville: Westminster John Knox, 2004.

Bishara, Marwan. *The Invisible Arab: The Promise and Peril of the Arab Revolutions*. New York: Nation Books, 2013.

Blackaby, Henry T., and Claude V. King. *Experiencing God: Knowing and Doing the Will of God*. Revised edition. Nashville: LifeWay Press, 1993.

Boesak, Allan Aubrey. *Dare We Speak of Hope? Searching for a Language of Life in Faith and Politics*. Grand Rapids: Eerdmans, 2014.

Brueggemann, Walter. *Cadences of Home: Preaching among Exiles*. Louisville: Westminster John Knox, 1997.

————. *The Prophetic Imagination*. 2nd edition. Minneapolis: Fortress, 2001.

Bulliet, Richard W. *Conversion to Islam in the Medieval Period: An Essay in Quantitative History*. Cambridge: Harvard University Press, 1979.

Deleuze, Gilles, and Felix Guattari. *A Thousand Plateaus: Capitalism and Schizophrenia*. Translated by Brian Massumi. 11th edition. Minneapolis: University of Minnesota Press, 2005. [Original English translation, 1987; original French edition, 1980.]

Donner, Fred McGraw, ed. *The Expansion of the Early Islamic State*. The Formation of the Classical Islamic World 5. Aldershot: Ashgate, 2008.

Doran, Robert, Leander E. Keck, J. Clinton McCann Jr., and Carol A. Newsom. *The New Interpreter's Commentary*, Volume 4. Nashville: Abingdon Press, 1996.

Durie, Mark. *The Third Choice: Islam, Dhimmitude and Freedom*. Melbourne: Deror Books, 2010.

Griffen, Wendell L. *The Fierce Urgency of Prophetic Hope*. Valley Forge: Judson, 2017.

Guinness, Os. *The Call: Finding and Fulfilling the Central Purpose of Your Life*. Nashville: W Publishing Group, 2003.

Jenkins, Philip. *The Lost History of Christianity*. New York: Harper Collins, 2011.

Khater, Akram Fouad. *Inventing Home: Emigration, Gender, and the Middle Class in Lebanon, 1870–1920*. Berkeley: University of California Press, 2001.

McGrath, Alister. *Evangelicalism and the Future of Christianity.* London: Hodder & Stoughton, 1994.

Moltmann, Jürgen. *Theology of Hope.* New York: Harper & Row, 1967.

Mulholland, M. Robert. *Shaped by the Word: The Power of Scripture in Spiritual Formation.* Revised edition. Nashville: Upper Room Books, 2000.

Munayer, Salim, and Lisa Loden. *The Land Cries Out.* Eugene: Wipf & Stock, 2012.

O'Connor, Kathleen. *Lamentations and the Tears of the World.* New York: Orbis, 2003.

Packer, J. I. *The Evangelical Anglican Identity Problem.* Oxford: Latimer House, 1978.

Pistone, Michele R., and John J. Hoeffner. *Stepping Out of the Brain Drain: Applying Catholic Social Teaching in a New Era of Migration.* Lanham: Lexington Books, 2007.

Reisacher, Evelyne. *Toward Respectful Understanding and Witness among Muslims: Essays in Honor of J. Dudley Woodberry.* Pasadena: William Carey Library, 2015.

Stott, John. *Evangelical Truth.* Leicester: IVP, 1999.

Volf, Miroslav, Prince Ghazi bin Muhammad bin Talal, and Melissa Yarrington, eds. *A Common Word: Muslims and Christians on Loving God and Neighbor.* Grand Rapids: Eerdmans, 2009.

Willard, Dallas, and Jan Johnson. *Hearing God: Developing a Conversational Relationship with God.* Updated and expanded edition. Downers Grove: IVP Books, 2012.

Yogarajah, Godfrey. "Disinformation, Discrimination, Destruction and Growth: A Case Study on Persecution of Christians in Sri Lanka." *International Journal for Religious Freedom* 1, no. 1 (2008): 85–94.

Contributors

Dr Martin Accad is the Chief Academic Officer of the Arab Baptist Theological Seminary (ABTS) in Mansourieh, Lebanon, and Director of the Institute of Middle East Studies (IMES) located at ABTS. He is also Associate Professor of Islamic Studies at ABTS and Fuller Theological Seminary, Pasadena, California, USA. In addition, he is Director of Programs, Middle East, for the Centre on Religion and Global Affairs (www.crga.org.uk). He gave the keynote paper on "Minoritization."

Jonathan Andrews is British and lives in the UK. He has been researching and writing on the Middle East since 2003. His focus is on the issues that underlie the day-to-day lives of Middle Eastern Christian communities. He has a master's in Global Issues in Contemporary Mission from Redcliffe College, UK. He is the author of two books (see Bibliography) and the editor of this one.

Ramez Atallah is the General Secretary of the Bible Society of Egypt, a post he has held since 1990. He was born and raised in Egypt. He moved with his parents to Canada in the early 1960s after the Egyptian government nationalized his parents' properties. He returned to Egypt in 1980, together with his wife, Rebecca, who is Canadian although born in Haiti where her parents were missionaries. He was Regional Secretary for the Middle East of the International Fellowship of Evangelical Students (IFES) from 1980 to 1990. He has participated in the Lausanne Movement since its inception in 1974, twice serving as its Vice-Chairman, and was Program Chairman for the Cape Town 2010 Congress. He gave the keynote paper on "Persecution and Suffering."

Daniel Bannoura is a member of the faculty of Bethlehem Bible College where he is an instructor in Comparative Religion and Church History. He was born in Jerusalem and grew up in Palestine and the USA. He has a bachelor's degree in Physics from the University of Florida and holds master's degrees in Theology from the London School of Theology and in Islamic Philosophy from the University of Chicago. His academic interests cover medieval philosophy, Arab theology and Muslim–Christian relations. He gave the critical reflection on "Persecution and Suffering."

Greg Butt is Canadian and pastor of Northmount Baptist Church in Calgary, Canada. He was born in Calgary but spent much of his childhood in India where his parents were missionaries. He holds a Bachelor of Biblical Studies (Briercrest Bible College, 1984), a Master of Divinity (Ambrose Seminary, formerly Canadian Theological Seminary, 1988) and a master's degree in Christian Leadership (Crest Leadership, December 2017). He gave the global cross-check on "Emigration."

Elie Haddad is President of the Arab Baptist Theological Seminary (ABTS) in Mansourieh, Lebanon. He grew up in Sidon, Lebanon, before moving to Canada where he lived, worked and studied for fifteen years. He returned to Lebanon in 2005 when he joined the staff of ABTS. He became President in 2008. He holds Canadian and Lebanese nationality. He gave the keynote paper on "Emigration."

Philip Halliday is a British citizen born in northern Scotland. He is a Baptist minister and has lived in France since 1993. He was Baptist Mission Society's Regional Director for Europe, the Middle East and North Africa until summer 2017. He combined this with leading the French Baptists' church-planting team. Since September 2017 he has focused on local church-planting in France as well as continuing as Head of Development for the French Baptist Federation. He gave the global cross-check on "Minoritization."

Dr Nehla Issac is Syrian and lives in Damascus. Her first degree was in dentistry and after working for several years she became an Assistant Professor of Dentistry at the University of Damascus. In 2001 she founded Women Above Crisis, a charity supporting women in difficult situations. In 2006 the service expanded to include young men and cooperation with IFES. In 2015 she became head of a charity offering humanitarian and relief services, including psychological support, to victims of the war in Syria. She gave the critical reflection on "Hopelessness and Despair."

Dr Yohanna Katanacho is Professor of Biblical Studies and Academic Dean at Nazareth Evangelical College. He is of Arab/Palestinian ethnicity and Israeli nationality. He gave the keynote paper on "Hopelessness and Despair." His presence was via online connectivity because Israeli nationals are not allowed entry to Lebanon.

Dr Ehab el-Kharrat is a medical doctor in Egypt. His work includes establishing an organization that works with drug addicts. He is an elder of Qasr al-Dūbārah Presbyterian Church, Cairo, and a former member of the upper house of the

Egyptian Parliament. He gave the critical reflection on "Minoritization" and also the introductory presentation.

Shane McNary is an American citizen living and working in Slovakia, primarily among Roma peoples. He gave the global cross-check on "Hopelessness and Despair."

Dr Gary Nelson is Canadian and President of Tyndale University College and Seminary in Toronto, Canada. He gave a series of devotional addresses each taken from the book of Psalms. This material is interspersed throughout the book.

Rev Dr Helen Paynter is a British citizen and Principal of Bristol Baptist College (UK). She gave a personal reflection on "Hopelessness and Despair."

Rev Harout Seliman is a Syrian working in Aleppo. Ethnically, he is of Armenian origin and is a priest in the Armenian Evangelical Churches in the Near East. He holds a bachelor's degree in Theology and a master's in Theology of Ministry, both from the Near East School of Theology in Beirut, Lebanon. Among various positions held he has been Chair of the Educational Committee of the Armenian Evangelical Community in Syria from 1998 to the present day. He gave the critical reflection on "Emigration."

Gordon Showell-Rogers is Global Director of One We Stand (http://onewestand.org/) which promotes religious freedom and social justice. He was Associate Secretary General of the World Evangelical Alliance from 2010 to 2016, having previously been General Secretary of the European Evangelical Alliance for eleven years. Before that he taught in a high school, was on the leadership and staff of a local church in the UK, was General Secretary of the Austrian IFES movement and led a mission agency serving foreign students. He gave the global cross-check on "Persecution and Suffering."

Index

*Entries marked with an asterisk * also appear in the Glossary*

Langham Literature and its imprints are a ministry of Langham Partnership.

Langham Partnership is a global fellowship working in pursuit of the vision God entrusted to its founder John Stott –

> *to facilitate the growth of the church in maturity and Christ-likeness through raising the standards of biblical preaching and teaching.*

Our vision is to see churches in the majority world equipped for mission and growing to maturity in Christ through the ministry of pastors and leaders who believe, teach and live by the Word of God.

Our mission is to strengthen the ministry of the Word of God through:
- nurturing national movements for biblical preaching
- fostering the creation and distribution of evangelical literature
- enhancing evangelical theological education

especially in countries where churches are under-resourced.

Our ministry

Langham Preaching partners with national leaders to nurture indigenous biblical preaching movements for pastors and lay preachers all around the world. With the support of a team of trainers from many countries, a multi-level programme of seminars provides practical training, and is followed by a programme for training local facilitators. Local preachers' groups and national and regional networks ensure continuity and ongoing development, seeking to build vigorous movements committed to Bible exposition.

Langham Literature provides majority world preachers, scholars and seminary libraries with evangelical books and electronic resources through publishing and distribution, grants and discounts. The programme also fosters the creation of indigenous evangelical books in many languages, through writer's grants, strengthening local evangelical publishing houses, and investment in major regional literature projects, such as one volume Bible commentaries like *The Africa Bible Commentary* and *The South Asia Bible Commentary*.

Langham Scholars provides financial support for evangelical doctoral students from the majority world so that, when they return home, they may train pastors and other Christian leaders with sound, biblical and theological teaching. This programme equips those who equip others. Langham Scholars also works in partnership with majority world seminaries in strengthening evangelical theological education. A growing number of Langham Scholars study in high quality doctoral programmes in the majority world itself. As well as teaching the next generation of pastors, graduated Langham Scholars exercise significant influence through their writing and leadership.

To learn more about Langham Partnership and the work we do visit **langham.org**